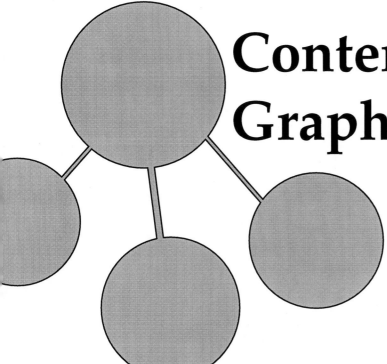

Content-Area Graphic Organizers

SOCIAL STUDIES

Margaret Cleveland

WALCH PUBLISHING

1   2   3   4   5   6   7   8   9   10

ISBN 0-8251-5007-8

Copyright © 2005

J. Weston Walch, Publisher

P. O. Box 658 • Portland, Maine 04104-0658

walch.com

Printed in the United States of America

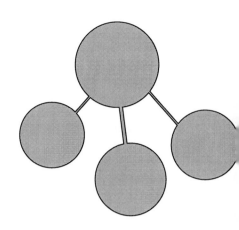

Table of Contents

To the Teacher . . . . *v*

Part 1: Graphic Organizer Overview 1

Lesson 1: Introduction to Graphic Organizers 3

Part 2: Graphic Organizers in Social Studies 5

Lesson 2: Organizing and Classifying 7
• Concept/Event Maps • Main Idea and Details Charts
• Hierarchy Diagrams • Spider Maps

Lesson 3: Sequencing 23
• Time Lines • Sequence Chains • Escalator Graphs

Lesson 4: Comparing and Contrasting 34
• Then and Now Charts • Venn Diagrams • Comparison Matrixes

Lesson 5: Showing Cause and-Effect 44
• Cause and Effect Maps •Problem/Solution Charts • Event Maps

Lesson 6: Writing 54
• KWL Charts • Note-Taking Organizers • Formal Outlines
• Informal Outlines • Expository Writing Organizers

Part 3: Reproducible Graphic Organizers 73

Answer Key 93

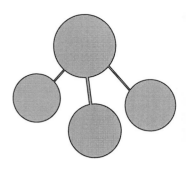

To the Teacher

Graphic organizers can be a versatile tool in your classroom. Organizers offer an easy, straightforward way to visually present a wide range of material. Research suggests that graphic organizers support learning in the classroom for all levels of learners. Gifted students, students on grade level, and students with learning difficulties all benefit from their use. Graphic organizers reduce the cognitive demand on students by helping them access information quickly and clearly. Using graphic organizers, learners can understand content more clearly and can take clear, concise notes. Ultimately, learners find it easier to retain and apply what they've learned.

Graphic organizers help foster higher-level thinking skills. They help students identify main ideas and details in their reading. They make it easier for students to see patterns, such as cause and effect, comparing and contrasting, and chronological order. Organizers also help learners master critical-thinking skills by asking them to recall, evaluate, synthesize, analyze, and apply what they've learned. Research suggests that graphic organizers contribute to better test scores because they help students understand relationships between key ideas and enable them to be more focused as they study.

This book shows students how they can use some common graphic organizers as they read and write in social studies classes. As they become familiar with graphic organizers, they will be able to adapt them to suit their needs.

In the social studies classroom, graphic organizers help students to
- preview new material
- make connections between new material and prior learning
- recognize patterns and main ideas in reading
- understand the relationships between key ideas
- organize information and take notes
- review material

This book offers graphic organizers suitable for social studies tasks, grouped according to big-picture skills, such as organizing and classifying information; sequencing; comparing and contrasting; showing cause and effect; and writing. Each organizer is introduced with an explanation of its primary uses and structure. Next comes a step-by-step description of how to create the organizer, with a completed example that uses text relevant to the content area. Finally, an application section asks students to use the techniques they have just learned to complete a blank organizer with information from a sample text. Throughout, learners are encouraged to customize the organizers to suit their needs. To emphasize the variety of graphic organizers available, an additional organizer suitable for each big-picture skill is introduced briefly at the end of each lesson.

Content-Area Graphic Organizers: Social Studies is easy to use. Simply photocopy and distribute the section on each graphic organizer. Blank copies of the graphic organizers are included at the back of this book so that you can copy them as often as needed. The blank organizers are also available for download at our web site, walch.com.

As learners become familiar with using graphic organizers, they will develop their own approaches and create their own organizers. Encourage them to adapt them, change them, and create their own for more complex strategies and connections.

Remember, there is no one right way to use graphic organizers; the best way is the way that works for each student.

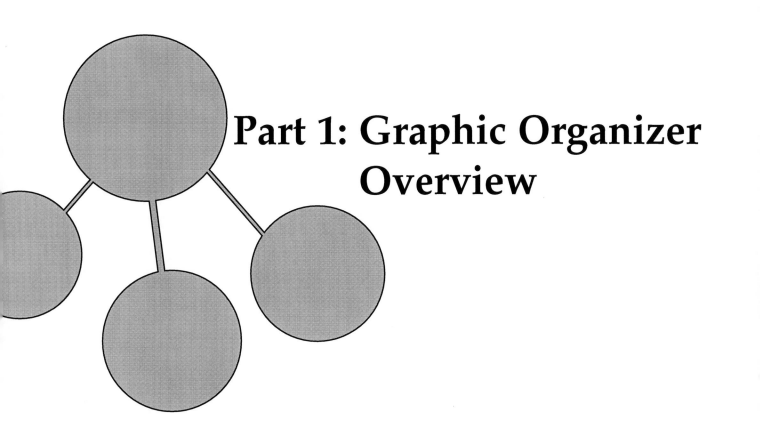

Part 1: Graphic Organizer Overview

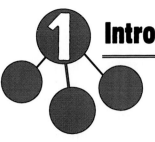

Introduction to Graphic Organizers

You've probably heard the old saying, "A picture is worth a thousand words." Like most old sayings, it isn't always true. But in many things we do, words alone are not the best way to communicate. That's why we use pictures and, in particular, graphic organizers.

A graphic organizer is simply a special drawing that contains words or numbers. If you've ever made a web or filled in a chart, then you already know how to use a graphic organizer. In this book, you'll find that you can use graphic organizers in ways you may not have expected. And you'll find that they can make your learning a lot easier!

The power of a graphic organizer is that instead of just telling you about relationships among things, it can show them to you. A graphic organizer can help you understand information much more easily than the same information written out as a paragraph of text. For example, look at this listing of names, addresses, and telephone numbers. Use it to find the telephone number for Amanda Jones.

Alden E. Jones, 18 Milford St., Boston, MA 02118, (617) 555-8040. Alun Huw Jones, 91 Westland Ave., Boston, MA 02115, (617) 555-9654. Alvin Jones, 715 Tremont St., Boston, MA 02118, (617) 555-2856. Alvin D. Jones, 77 Salem St., Boston, MA 02113, (617) 555-2890. Amanda Jones, 111 W. 8th St., Boston, MA 02127, (617) 555-0738. Amos K. Jones, 11 Helen St., Boston, MA 02124, (617) 555-3560. Andre N. Jones, 523 Mass. Ave., Boston, MA 02118, (617) 555-0829. Andrew Jones, 168 Northampton St., Boston, MA 02118, (617) 555-0069.

In order to find Amanda's number, you had to read, or at least scan, the whole text. Here is the same information presented in a graphic organizer—a table.

Name	Address	City, State, Zip	Phone
Alden E. Jones	18 Milford St.	Boston, MA 02118	(617) 555-8040
Alun Huw Jones	91 Westland Ave.	Boston, MA 02115	(617) 555-9654
Alvin Jones	715 Tremont St.	Boston, MA 02118	(617) 555-2856
Alvin D. Jones	77 Salem St.	Boston, MA 02113	(617) 555-2890
Amanda Jones	111 W. 8th St.	Boston, MA 02127	(617) 555-0738
Amos K. Jones	11 Helen St.	Boston, MA 02124	(617) 555-3560
Andre N. Jones	523 Mass Ave.	Boston, MA 02118	(617) 555-0829
Andrew Jones	168 Northampton St.	Boston, MA 02118	(617) 555-0069

Which arrangement was easier to use? Most people find it easier to see the information in the table. This is because the table gives all the names in one column, all the telephone numbers in another column, and all the information about each person in one row. As soon as you know how the table is set up—the labels at the top of each column tell you—you can quickly find what you're looking for.

Graphic organizers use lines, circles, grids, charts, tree diagrams, symbols, and other visual elements to show relationships—classifications, comparisons, contrasts, time sequence, parts of a whole, and so on—much more directly than text alone.

You can use graphic organizers in many ways. You can use them before you begin a lesson to lay the foundation for new ideas. They can help you recall what you already know about a subject and see how new material is connected to what you already know.

You can use them when you are reading to take notes or to keep track of what you read. It doesn't matter what you are reading—a textbook, a biography, or an informational article. Organizers can help you understand and analyze what you read. You can use them to recognize patterns in the reading. They can help you identify the main idea and its supporting details. They can help you compare and contrast all kinds of things, from people to ideas, animals, places, eras, and events.

Graphic organizers can help you after you read. You can use them to organize your notes and figure out the most important points in what you read. They are a great tool as you review to make sure you understood everything or as you prepare for a test.

You can use graphic organizers when you write, too. They are particularly useful for prewriting and planning. Organizers can help you brainstorm new ideas. They can help you sort out the key points you want to make. Graphic organizers can help you write clearly and precisely.

Think of graphic organizers as a new language. Using this new language may be a bit awkward at first, but once you gain some fluency, you'll enjoy communicating in a new way.

4

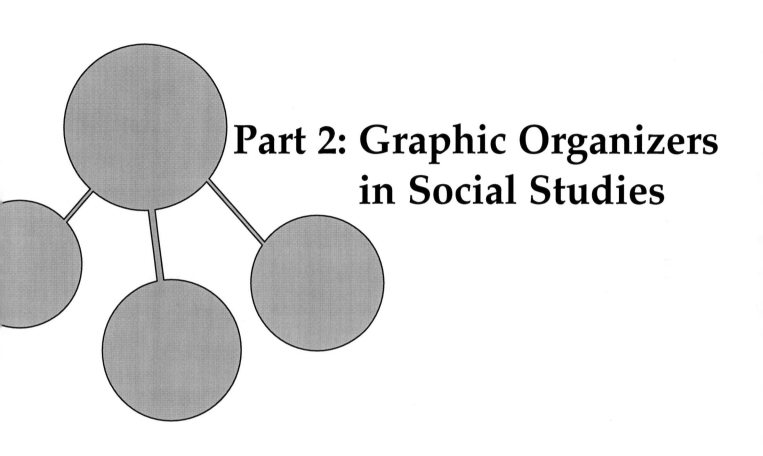

Part 2: Graphic Organizers in Social Studies

Organizing and Classifying

Imagine that you are going to the library to select a book. When you arrive, you find that books on the shelves are all mixed up. There are novels alongside encyclopedias. Books on the geography and history of the states are next to books about mountain lions. There is no order to the books at all. How will you find what you need?

Now think about how you categorize your assignments. What if your list of homework for one week looked like this:

- read pages 51–78
- write essay as assigned in class
- learn vocabulary words on page 44
- do problems from class worksheet
- memorize definitions from class notebook

How would you remember what books to read? How would you know which class worksheet to do? When you create a list, do you organize your homework assignments into categories with assigned headings? Look at the revised list of assignments below. Does it make more sense?

- Social Studies: read pages 51–78
- English: write essay as assigned in class
- Spanish: learn vocabulary words on page 44
- Math: do problems from class worksheet
- Science: memorize definitions from class notebook

The most important part of making a list is not that you are writing things down, but that you are organizing and classifying the information in your list. We organize and classify every day. In the library, we find books shelved by category. In our own notebooks, we find our assignments arranged by subject. If not, we would spend a lot of time looking for things or trying to figure out what things mean. Organizing and classifying is a skill you use when you read social studies material. When you read, you can look for patterns or ways to organize or classify, just as you would when you write down your assignments. In this lesson, we will look at three different ways to classify or organize information.

Concept/Event Maps

Every article you read for social studies—whether it is part of a textbook or a primary source—involves a main concept or event. Usually you can figure out the main concept by looking at the title or reading the introductory paragraph. Where a lot of people run into trouble is sorting out the key points that describe the main concept or event. A concept/event map can help you sort out the key points.

Using Concept/Event Maps

A concept/event map uses the questions who, what, where, when, how, and why to identify the key points. Once you can answer these questions about the article you are reading, you will know the key points.

In a concept/event map, you write the main idea (an event or a concept) in the middle of the page. Then you write the key questions around the main idea. On lines drawn out from the center, write the key facts that explain who, what, where, when, how, and why.

Concept/Event Maps in Action

Look at the article below about the life of Thomas Jefferson. Then see how a sample concept/event map is filled out on page 9.

Architect, Thinker, President

Many historians consider Thomas Jefferson one of the most influential people in our nation's history. He was a brilliant thinker, writer, and architect. He became the third president of the United States. His actions before and after his presidency continue to influence America today.

In 1776, when he was just thirty-three years old, Jefferson revised a very sketchy document for the Continental Congress. That document became the Declaration of Independence. Jefferson believed in freedom above all else. He drafted a bill that outlined religious freedom for those in his native state of Virginia. This bill became a foundation document for the later Bill of Rights.

After the American Revolution, Jefferson became minister to France. This was an important time in French history, as it was the eve of their violent revolution. The fight between nobles and peasants captured the interest of many Americans. Some sympathized with the nobles. Others, like Jefferson, sympathized with the peasants who wanted more freedom. Leaders in America were split on their sympathies. This split led to the formation of two rival political parties. The Federalists became the more conservative party in America, and the Democratic Republicans were more liberal—they sympathized with French peasants. Jefferson was the leader of the Republicans.

In 1800, Jefferson became president—reluctantly. His presidency was marked by some controversy, including his purchase of the land area known as the Louisiana Territory. However, the Louisiana Purchase turned out to be one of the most critical decisions of his presidency. This purchase doubled the size of the United States.

When his term of presidency was over, Jefferson retired to his home, known as Monticello. There he sketched the architectural plans for the

University of Virginia, which stands today as a monument to Jefferson's remarkable talents. Fittingly, Thomas Jefferson died on Independence Day—July 4, 1826.

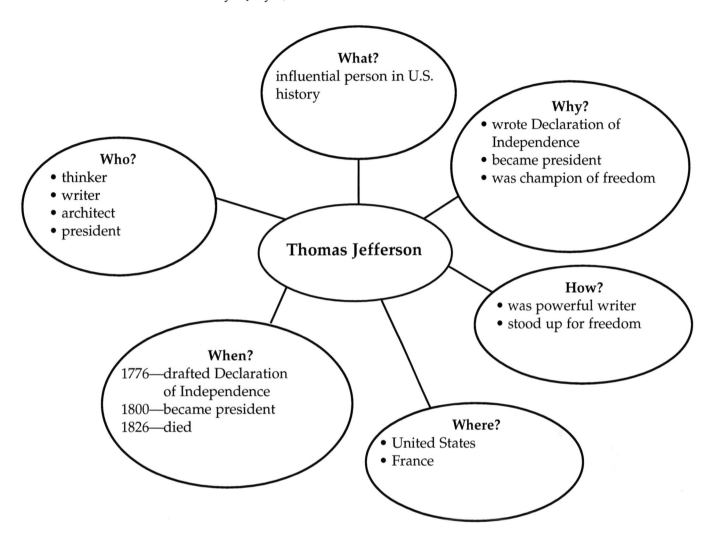

Application Now it's your turn to create a concept/event map. Read the passage below about the Louisiana Purchase. As you read, think about who, what why, how, where, and when. Then complete the graphic organizer on page 11.

Double the Country

Historians still consider the decision to buy the Louisiana Territory an important turning point in American history. This decision doubled the size of the United States, making the United States one of the largest countries in the world.

In 1803, Thomas Jefferson was the third president of the United States. The area known as the Louisiana Territory belonged to France, under the leadership of the Emperor Napoleon. The price tag was $15 million.

Today, $15 million might buy one skyscraper in a midsized American city. East to west, the Louisiana Territory included all the land from the Mississippi River to the Rocky Mountains. It also extended north and south from Canada to the Mexican border, including most of the land that today makes up Texas and New Mexico. It included the land that is now Arkansas, Colorado, Iowa, Kansas, Louisiana, Minnesota, Missouri, Montana, Nebraska, North Dakota, Oklahoma, South Dakota, and Wyoming.

When Napoleon offered the Louisiana Territory to the United States, President Jefferson really wanted to buy it. But there was no provision in the newly written U.S. Constitution that authorized the purchase of new land. Because Jefferson wanted to abide strictly by the law of the Constitution, he was reluctant to buy the land. Yet, the consequences of not buying the land far outweighed his worries about the purchase being unconstitutional. He decided to buy the land. The Senate agreed with him, and Congress gave Jefferson the money to buy the land.

In 1803, no one knew how far-reaching the consequences of buying the land would be. Jefferson knew that he wanted the port of New Orleans because it was a destination point for farmers of the Ohio Valley to sell and trade their crops. But beyond New Orleans, the land included in the Louisiana Purchase turned out to be fertile farmland as well as a source of many natural resources. The Louisiana Purchase ended up contributing significantly to the U.S. economy, not only doubling the size of the country, but making it much richer and more powerful than it had been.

Even though the Louisiana Purchase was not officially allowed by the Constitution, Jefferson chose to interpret the law of the land in a broad sense. But to make sure that it would be possible to continue to acquire new lands, in 1828, the U.S. Supreme Court upheld the constitutionality of Jefferson's decision. Also, the Court ruled to add a clause to the Constitution about acquiring land.

10

Concept/Event Map Answer the who, what, why, how, where, and when questions about the passage you have just read on the Louisiana Purchase. Then complete the map below to help you remember the key points of the article. When you go back to study about this topic, or any topic for which you use a concept/event map, the main ideas will be well organized and easy to study and remember.

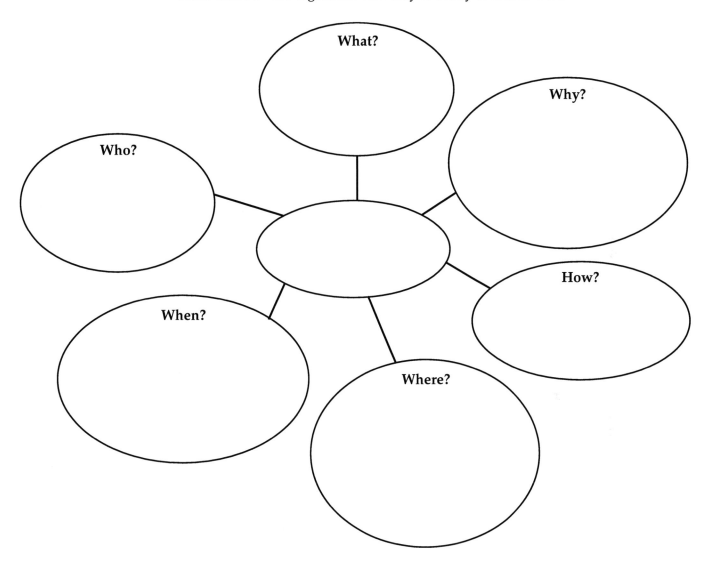

Main Idea and Details Charts

Have you ever read something and found that the writing rambled on without ever stating the main idea of the article? It's hard to remember the facts when you don't see how they are connected to a main idea or central thought.

Every well-written article is organized around a main idea supported by details that illustrate that idea. Most of the time the main idea is stated in the title or in the opening paragraph. That makes it fairly easy to spot. However, sometimes the main idea is not clear. For example, when you read a document or a primary source, you may not be able to identify the main idea very easily. Then you have to ask yourself these two questions:

- How would I summarize this article in one sentence?

- What title would I give this article?

Next you want to identify the supporting details. Sometimes there are several details in an article or in a primary source. Your job is to figure out which are the most important details that support the main idea. To do this, you can ask yourself these two questions:

- Does this detail broaden my understanding of the main idea? (yes or no)

- In what way does this detail broaden my understanding of the main idea?

Using Main Idea and Details Charts

A great way to cull information from an article is to create a main idea and details chart as you read. You can use it to take notes so that you are not overwhelmed with less important details. You can also use it to review the text when you write a paper or take a test. A main idea and details chart will help you remember the key points of your reading.

There are several versions of a main idea and details chart. For social studies, it is helpful to use a graphic organizer that shows how the details add up to the main idea.

Main Idea and Details Charts in Action

Read the short primary source letter below from Rose Greenhow, a Civil War spy who was caught and put in prison. This letter describes her feelings about her arrest and imprisonment. See if you can determine the main idea and the details before you look at the filled-in chart that follows the letter. Remember to ask yourself the main idea questions and detail questions to determine what you think should go in the chart. (Note: The spelling is as Rose Greenhow originally wrote it.)

Washington, Nov. 17th, 1861,

To the Hon. Wm. H. Seward,
Secretary of State:

Sir—For nearly three months I have been confined, a close prisoner, shut out from air and exercise, and denied all communication with family and friends.

"Patience is said to be a great virtue," and I have practised it to my utmost capacity of endurance. . . .

I therefore most respectfully submit, that on Friday, August 23d, without warrant or other show of authority, I was arrested by the Detective Police, and my house taken in charge by them; that all my private letters, and my papers of a life time, were read and examined by them; that every law of decency was violated in the search of my house and person. . . .

My object is to call your attention to the fact: that during this long imprisonment, I am yet ignorant of the causes of my arrest; that my house has been seized . . . that the valuable furniture it contained has been abused and destroyed; that during some periods of my imprisonment I have suffered greatly for want of proper and sufficient food. . . .

The "iron heel of power" may keep down, but it cannot crush out, the spirit of resistance in a people armed for the defence of their rights; and I tell you now, sir, that you are standing over a crater, whose smothered fires in a moment may burst forth. . . .

In conclusion, I respectfully ask your attention to this protest, and have the honor to be, &c.,

(Signed)
Rose O. N. Greenhow

Here is the filled-in chart, showing how the main idea and details are organized.

Supporting Detail: Greenhow was arrested without a warrant.

+

Supporting Detail: Greenhow does not know why she was arrested.

+

Supporting Detail: Greenhow has been badly treated and will not tolerate her rights being violated.

=

The Main Idea: Rose Greenhow is writing to the Secretary of State because she believes she is being held in prison unjustly and she feels her rights have been violated.

Application Now it's your turn. Create a main idea and details chart based on the diary entry that follows. It was written in 1889 by Lucy Larcom. At the age of eleven, Lucy went to work in the textile mills in Lowell, Massachusetts. Read the article. Ask yourself the questions about the main idea:

- How would I summarize this article in one sentence?

- What title would I give this article?

Then examine the supporting details and ask yourself:

- Does this detail broaden my understanding of the main idea?

- In what way does this detail broaden my understanding of the main idea?

From Lucy Larcom's Diary

So I went to my first day's work in the mill with a light heart. The novelty of it made it seem easy, and it really was not hard, just to change the bobbins on the spinning-frames every three quarters of an hour or so, with half a dozen other little girls who were doing the same thing. When I came back at night, the family began to pity me for my long, tiresome day's work, but I laughed and said,—

"Why, it is nothing but fun. It is just like play."

And for a little while it was only a new amusement; I liked it better than going to school and "making believe" I was learning when I was not. . . .

There were compensations for being shut in to daily toil so early. The mill itself had its lessons for us. But it was not, and could not be, the right sort of life for a child, and we were happy in the knowledge that, at the longest, our employment was only to be temporary. . . .

In the older times it was seldom said to little girls, as it always has been said to boys, that they ought to have some definite plan, while they were children, what to be and do when they were grown up. There was usually but one path open before them, to become good wives and housekeepers. . . . When I was growing up, they had already begun to be encouraged to do so. We were often told that it was our duty to develop any talent we might possess, or at least to learn how to do some one thing which the world needed, or which would make it a pleasanter world. . . .

One great advantage which came to these many stranger girls through being brought together, away from their own homes, was that it taught them to go out of themselves, and enter into the lives of others. Home-life, when one always stays at home, is necessarily narrowing. . . . We have hardly begun to live until we can take in the idea of the whole human family as the one to which we truly belong. To me, it was an incalculable help to find myself among so many working girls, all of us thrown upon our own resources, but thrown much more upon each others' sympathies.

Main Idea and Details Chart

Fill in the main idea and details chart below. You may want to begin with the main idea first, then see what supporting details add up to it. Or, you may want to try putting the details on paper first, then seeing what they all add up to.

Supporting Detail:

+

Supporting Detail:

+

Supporting Detail:

=

The Main Idea:

Hierarchy Diagrams

Have you ever tried to describe your family to another person? Did you include your aunts and uncles, brothers and sisters, cousins, nieces and nephews? It can be complicated to explain who is who, especially in a big family. Luckily, there is a tool called a family tree. This tool can help you visualize the people in a family and how they are related to one another.

A family tree is a type of hierarchy diagram. A hierarchy is a series of ranked people, things, or groups within a system. A hierarchy diagram illustrates this ordered ranking. In a family tree, for example, the grandparents would be on one level. Their children would be on a level below, and their children on a level below that, and so on. Here's what a family tree might look like:

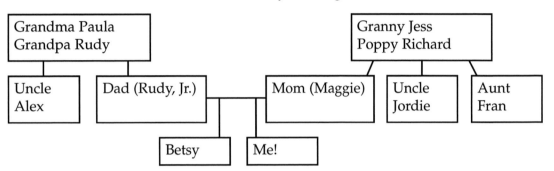

In a family tree hierarchy diagram, the oldest generation is on top. The next grouping is the second generation, or the next oldest. The last grouping is the youngest generation. They appear at the bottom of the diagram.

In social studies and in history, you will often see hierarchy diagrams. They are used in textbooks describing family trees, branches of government—both local and national—and historical events. You will also see hierarchy diagrams that describe company organizational charts or the structure of computer programs or scientific categories.

Using Hierarchy Diagrams

You may want to use a hierarchy diagram when you recognize that an article or a part of a text explains how things are related to one another in an ordered way. This means the most important (in rank, age, status, and so forth) is on the top. The second in importance is in the next level, and so on, down to the least important. "Important" doesn't mean essential or necessary; it means lesser in status according to rank, age, or position.

When you are reading an article, look for certain words as cues that a hierarchy diagram might be the best way to organize your notes. Here are some words and phrases to look for:

at the top of	most important	oversees
underneath	ranked by	directs
supported by	key people or events	in charge of

If you see words like these, you can sketch out a hierarchy diagram to organize the information you are reading.

Hierarchy Diagrams in Action

Below is an article about how three types of local city governments work. After the article are three different hierarchy diagrams that show the three types of local government. Note that in each case the strongest or most important in rank is at the top of the diagram. The least important in rank is at the bottom. Look for some of the key phrases to see how they translate into the hierarchy diagram.

Weak or Strong or None at All

Do you have a weak mayor? Or do you have a strong mayor? Maybe you don't have a mayor at all. Whatever your local government, the most important people who run the city are the voters who elect their representatives.

A weak mayor doesn't really mean that the mayor isn't a good mayor. The weak mayoral system is a name given to a form of local government in which voters elect a mayor and a city council to run the town. Often the mayor is just a ceremonial role because the council does most of the decision-making for the town or city. Underneath the city council and the mayor are the department heads. Departments include public safety, public works, parks and recreation, and finance.

A strong mayoral system doesn't mean that the mayor is really strong, either. A strong mayoral system means that the city council advises the mayor, who makes many of the decisions for the town. The mayor is in charge of the department heads. They all report to the mayor and not to the city council, as in a weak mayoral system. In this system, voters elect the city council as well as the mayor.

A council-manager system has no mayor at all. This is a system often found in smaller towns. In this system, the city council oversees a city manager, and the city manager directs the department heads. In some ways the city manager is like a mayor, only he or she doesn't have the same authority as a mayor.

Discovering what lies beneath the politics of your town can help you make better decisions about how you want your town to run. As a voter, you will be glad you have all the correct information!

Here are the three completed hierarchy diagrams.

Weak Mayoral System

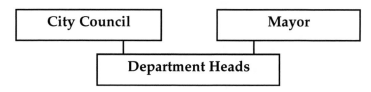

Strong Mayoral System

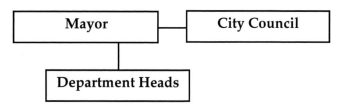

Council-Manager Government

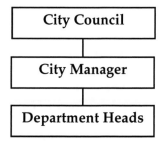

Application Now it's your turn to make a hierarchy diagram. Read through the following article about the branches of the federal government. Look for key words to help you determine what should go at the top of the diagram and what should go in the next tier. Then use this information to complete the blank chart on page 21.

A Balancing Act

The young men who wrote the Constitution of the United States had a tough job to do. Their job was to create a framework that would outline how the U.S. government would work. One of the most important issues they faced was how to make sure that no one person could ever have total control over the people. They had experienced government by a single ruler when they were ruled by the king of England.

So the men who wrote the Constitution created a system in which all the power in the government would be shared by three separate but equal branches. The system they devised is called the system of checks and balances. This means that each branch can reject the decisions of the other two. In this way, the branches can keep one another in check.

The framers first established the executive branch. This branch includes the President, the Vice President, and all the chief staff members advising these two people. These advisers are known as the cabinet. There are roughly fourteen cabinet positions; sometimes the President eliminates or adds a cabinet office, according to the needs of the country. For example, President George W. Bush created a new cabinet post in 2002, the Secretary of Homeland Security. That position had never before existed in the executive branch.

The legislative branch of government has the same authority as the executive branch. This branch includes all the members of the Senate (100) and all the members of the House of Representatives (435). Together these two groups are called the Congress. Their job is to write and review bills that may become laws. They then vote for or against these bills. Congress members don't always agree on what bills should become laws, so there is often a lot of discussion, debate, and revision of bills.

The judicial branch is made up of the courts. In the courts, judges decide how to apply and interpret the laws that are made by Congress. Sometimes the intent of the law is unclear, so the courts need to clarify the meaning.

The highest court in the judicial branch is called the Supreme Court. The judges who sit on this court make some of the most important decisions in the country. Each year, about 4,500 cases are sent to the Supreme Court. But each year, the judges only hear about 200 of them. The rest of the cases are settled at the next court level, the court of appeals. The lowest court level is called the district court.

These three branches of government are the backbone of the U.S. government. Ultimately, however, the voters choose the people to represent us in the government, so we must listen closely to elect those who will uphold the best interests for all U.S. citizens.

Hierarchy Diagram   After you have read the article about the three branches of the federal government, complete a hierarchy diagram that shows how the three branches are related to one another. Write the most important element at the top. Write less important elements lower down. Use lines to show relationships between elements. Add or delete boxes and lines as needed.

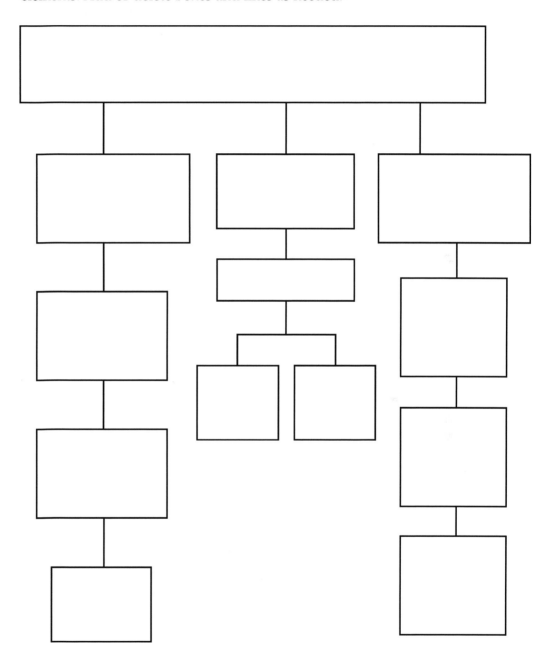

Spider Maps A spider map is another graphic organizer you can use to organize your reading notes. You can use a spider map any time you want to illustrate the main idea and details of a text.

Write the topic or theme of the reading in the oval. Write one main idea on each diagonal line. Write one supporting detail on each horizontal line. Add or delete lines as needed.

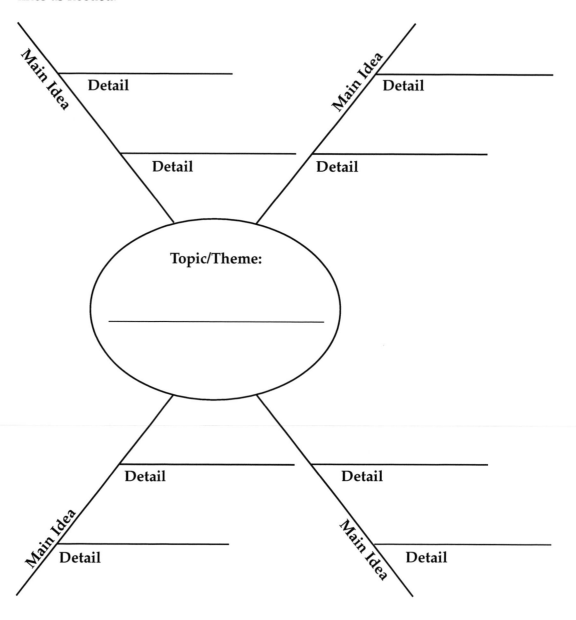

22

3 Sequencing

Have you ever had someone give you directions, but they gave them out of order? What happened? Did you get lost or have a hard time figuring out how to follow the directions?

Or imagine that you opened a cookbook and found that the recipe for chocolate chip cookies looked like this:

Recipe for Chocolate Chip Cookies

Cook for 25–30 minutes until the cookies are lightly browned.

Mix chocolate chips with flour, salt, and baking powder.

Pour in chocolate chips.

Add vanilla.

Cream together eggs and sugar.

Preheat oven to 350°.

If you followed the sequence of this recipe, you probably wouldn't make very good cookies!

Order of events, or sequencing, is a key pattern in social studies. When you study history, it is important to understand what happened first, next, then last. Understanding how things happened and in what order helps you understand why those things happened. For example, when Rosa Parks decided not to move to the back of the bus, she caused a ripple effect that eventually led to the boycott and integration of buses in Montgomery, Alabama. If you learned about these historic events out of order, they would not be as meaningful.

In this lesson, we will look closely at two graphic organizers that can help you recognize and understand sequencing. The first is a time line, which you have probably worked with before. The second is a sequence chain, which will show you the flow of events from one to another.

Time Lines

The study of history is often presented in chronological order. This means that it is presented in the order that the events occurred. When you read about history, you'll see that dates are often sprinkled throughout the text. But the dates don't mean much unless they are set in some kind of time frame. Time lines are a great way to organize information so that it follows chronological order.

Using Time Lines

Time lines come in many shapes and sizes. All time lines include a date and some type of slot to write in brief information about what happened on that date. Sometimes, instead of written information, time lines have pictures that represent the event or activity.

Some time lines are very detailed. Some are more general. For example, you could create a time line of the events in your classroom. Each day could be chronicled according to birthdays, holidays, sporting events, or other special activities. You might need the whole wall to cover the year. You could also create a time line of the highlights of the past twenty centuries. This time line might include four or five events per century, covering more than 2,000 years.

Almost any event or span of time can be shown with a time line. For example, you could create a detailed time line of your activities in the past week. What did you do each day? You could also create a time line of your whole life. What events would you want to highlight? Any time you are reading something that includes a time frame, a time line can help you keep the events or the ideas straight.

Time lines usually have the dates on one side and the events depicted on the other. Time lines can be horizontal, or they can be vertical. If they are vertical—going from top to bottom—usually the earliest events are placed on the bottom. Later events appear higher on the line, with the most recent events at the top. If the time line is horizontal, the earliest events usually are placed at the left side of the time line. Then the events progress to the most recent date, on the right.

Time Lines in Action The passage below describes the most important inventions created throughout history. Below the text, you'll see a time line that illustrates the key inventions. Note that this time line is very simple, and it covers a huge time frame.

Tools from Long Ago

Can you imagine life without a wheel? What if there were no signs or words printed on a page? Almost everything you do, every tool you use, was once the invention and innovation of a creative mind. Many of the articles we use today were created more than 2,000 years ago.

Do you know anyone who has false teeth? Do you know when false teeth were invented? It might surprise you to find out that false teeth have been around a lot longer than the telescope, the trumpet, or even paper. False teeth were the brainchild of the ancient Etruscans and were first used around 700 B.C.E.

Other B.C.E. inventions include the tent (40,000 B.C.E.), maps (3800 B.C.E.), soap (3000 B.C.E.), and the first flush toilet—invented way back in 2000 B.C.E. You probably think that ice cream is a twentieth-century invention. Would it surprise you to know it was invented in 400 B.C.E.? And kites have been around for more than 3,000 years. They were first invented in China, around 1000 B.C.E. The Chinese were also famous for inventing the umbrella—not to keep out the rain, but to keep out the bright sun. This invention happened around the same time as the kite. The Chinese also invented gunpowder, around 700 B.C.E., to propel rockets.

So the next time you go for a lick of ice cream, thank the ancients for it and for many other inventions that help us through the twenty-first century.

Inventions

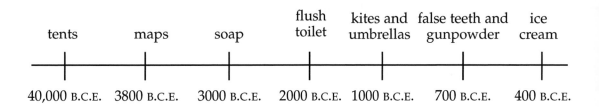

Application Now it's your turn to try your hand at a time line. Research one of the topics below. Then create a time line based on the facts you learn about the topic and its history. Feel free to use the time line provided on page 27, or create your own, using drawings or art from your sources.

1. The years of the American Revolution were filled with events that began the history of the young American republic. Research the events that led up to the American Revolution, and create a time line that reflects the key events.

2. Fashion in the twentieth century has changed as the times have changed. Research fashions for either men or women, and create a time line that shows the changing fashions.

3. Popular music in each decade of the twentieth century has changed to reflect the psyche of the American people. Find out what types of music were introduced at what times, and create a time line that reflects popular music changes.

4. Choose an artist of the nineteenth or twentieth century, and create a time line that shows the key events in his or her life.

5. Choose one decade in the settling of the West, and create a time line that shows key events during that decade.

6. The late nineteenth and twentieth centuries were times of major technological advances. Many inventions changed the way Americans work, play, and live. Create a time line that shows when key technologies were introduced to society.

7. Find out what happened on one day of the year at different periods of history, and plot the events on a time line. You might want to look at the newspaper, which often lists historical events for the day and the years that the events took place.

8. Create a time line that depicts the events in the life of your favorite author. Why is it interesting or important to know about these events?

9. Find out when the musical instruments of the orchestra were invented. Create a time line that shows the years of their invention.

10. Choose your favorite car maker, and create a time line that shows when various models were designed and put on the market.

Time Line Use the time line below to show the events from one of the projects on page 26. There's space here if you want to include a drawing or a picture to illustrate your time line. Put the earliest event at the bottom, with more recent events above, in the order in which they took place. The most recent event should be at the top.

Sequence Chains

Like time lines, sequence chains are a way to organize events in the order in which they occurred. Just as history is often written in time order, other social studies topics are written in sequential order. This means that events are linked to one another by the order in which they happened. Sequential order tells what happened first, next, and last.

Using Sequence Chains

The sequence chain can be used to describe a chain of events, stages of development, phases of an era, or actions taken by an individual or a group, as well as the outcomes of all of the steps in the sequence. When you are learning about a sequence, you want to ask yourself four key questions:

- What person, event, phase, project, or action is being discussed?

- What are the steps, actions, or events that describe this person or time period?

- How do these steps, actions, or events relate to one another?

- What is the final outcome of these events?

The last key question is very important. The answer indicates the importance of the subject.

Sequence Chains in Action

The following statements are from a letter Paul Revere wrote in 1798. In it, he describes his ride on April 8–9, 1775, as he set out to warn the Sons of Liberty that the British were coming. See how these statements are then graphed into a sequence chain.

The British Are Coming!

". . . if the British went out by Water, we should shew two Lanthorns in the North Church Steeple; and if by Land, one, as a Signal. . . ."

(Revere writes that if the British arrived in Boston by sea, a signal of two lights would be shown from the North Church. If they arrived by land, just one signal would be shown.)

"About 10 o'clock, Dr. Warren Sent in a great haste for me and begged that I would immediately Set off for Lexington, where Messrs. Hancock and Adams were. . . ."

(Dr. Warren, one of the Sons of Liberty, asked Revere to ride to where John Hancock and Samuel Adams were to warn them that the British were planning to arrest them.)

"When I got into town, I met Col. Conant and several others; they said that they had seen our signals. I told them what was Acting, and went to get me a Horse; I got a horse of Deacon Larkin."

(Revere borrowed a horse from his friend Deacon Larkin and began his ride to warn Hancock and Adams.)

". . . I awakened the Captain of the minute men; and after that I alarmed almost every house, till I got to Lexington. I found Messrs. Hancock and Adams at the Rev. Mr. Clark's; I told them my errand. . . . and set off for Concord. . . ."

(Revere rode from Boston to Lexington where he found Hancock and Adams. He told them they were in danger of being arrested. Then he started for Concord.)

"I was about one hundred Rods ahead when I saw two men. . . . In an Instant I was surrounded by four . . . the Major ordered . . . if I attempted to run, or anybody insulted them, to blow my brains out."

(Revere was caught by British soldiers.)

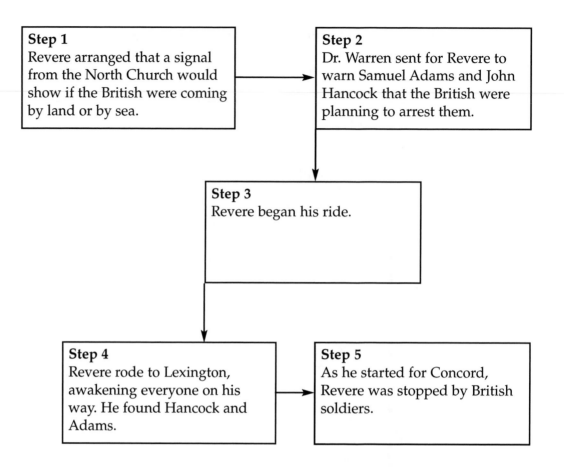

Step 1
Revere arranged that a signal from the North Church would show if the British were coming by land or by sea.

Step 2
Dr. Warren sent for Revere to warn Samuel Adams and John Hancock that the British were planning to arrest them.

Step 3
Revere began his ride.

Step 4
Revere rode to Lexington, awakening everyone on his way. He found Hancock and Adams.

Step 5
As he started for Concord, Revere was stopped by British soldiers.

Application The article below is adapted from *Ben's Guide to U.S. Government* (http://bensguide.gpo.gov), a service of the U.S. Government Printing Office. It describes how a law is made. As you read it, keep in mind the key questions listed on page 28. These questions will help you focus on the most important parts of the article. Then create a sequence chain based on the key points in the article. Hint: Look for the topic sentence in each of the paragraphs. These will often tell you which are the most important points.

How a Law Is Made

Laws are started in the legislative branch of the government. There are two parts to the legislative branch. A bill can be started in either chamber of Congress—the House of Representatives or the Senate.

When a representative has an idea for a new law, she or he becomes a sponsor of that bill. She or he introduces it by giving it to the clerk of the House or by placing it in a box, called the hopper. The clerk assigns a legislative number to the bill, with *H.R.* for bills introduced in the House of Representatives and *S.* for bills introduced in the Senate. The Government Printing Office (GPO) then prints the bill and distributes copies to each representative.

Next the speaker of the House assigns the bill to a committee for study. The House has twenty-two standing committees. . . . The standing committee (or often a subcommittee) studies the bill and hears testimony from experts and people interested in the bill. The committee then may release the bill with a recommendation to pass it. Or, they might revise the bill and release it, or lay it aside so that the House cannot vote on it. Releasing the bill is called reporting it out. Laying it aside is called tabling.

If the bill is released, it then goes on a calendar, which is a list of bills awaiting actions. Here the House Rules Committee may call for the bill to be voted on quickly, or may limit debate about the bill. Bills may be passed by unanimous consent, or by a two-thirds vote if members agree to suspend the rules.

The bill now goes to the floor of the House for consideration and begins with a complete reading of the bill. . . . If the bill passes by simple majority (218 of 435), the bill moves to the Senate.

Just as in the House, the bill then is assigned to a committee. It is assigned to one of the Senate's sixteen standing committees. . . . The Senate committee studies and either releases or tables the bill just like the House standing committee.

Once released, the bill goes to the Senate floor for consideration. Bills are voted on in the Senate based on the order they come from the committee. However, an urgent bill may be pushed ahead by leaders of the majority party. When the Senate considers the bill, they can debate about it for a very long time. When there is no more debate, the bill is voted on. A simple majority (51 of 100) passes the bill.

The bill now moves onto a conference committee, which is made up of members from each house. The committee works out any differences between the House and Senate versions of the bill. The revised bill is sent back to both houses for their final approval. Once approved, the bill is printed by the U.S. Government Printing Office in a process called enrolling. The clerk from the introducing house certifies the final version.

The enrolled bill is now signed by the speaker of the House and then by the Vice President. Finally, it is sent for presidential consideration. The President has ten days to sign or veto the enrolled bill. If the President vetoes the bill, it can still become a law if two-thirds of the Senate and two-thirds of the House then vote in favor of the bill.

Sequence Chain Simplify the article you just read into eight steps or parts of a sequence. Write phrases or words in the boxes to represent the eight actions that make a law. Notice how much easier it is to remember a sequence when you can see it laid out in clear steps.

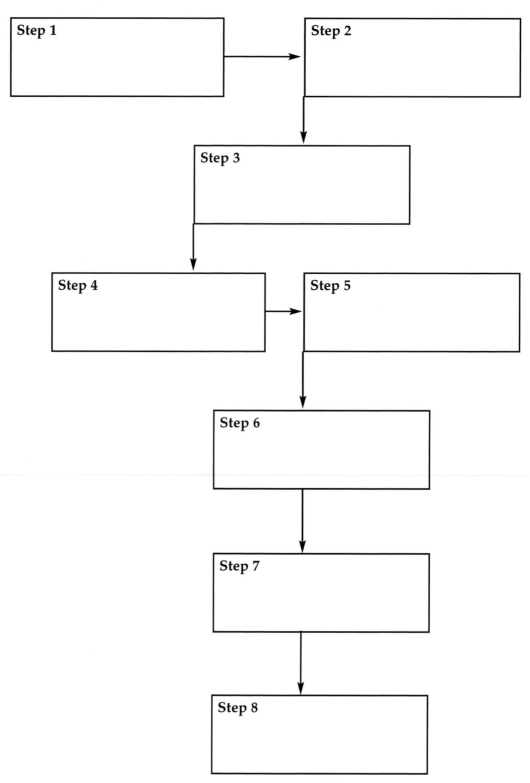

Step 1

Step 2

Step 3

Step 4

Step 5

Step 6

Step 7

Step 8

Escalator Graphs There are many other ways to track sequence in your reading. An escalator graph is useful to show the steps in a process, much like a sequence chain. At the bottom of the escalator graph, write the beginning event. At the top, write the final outcome. If you were charting the way a law is made, the introduction of the bill would be at the bottom, and the passage of a law would be at the top.

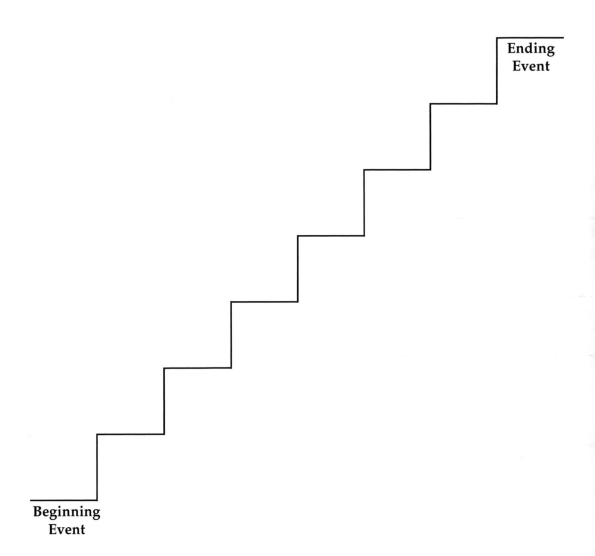

Ending Event

Beginning Event

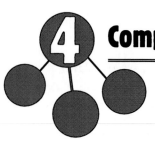

Comparing and Contrasting

What are your favorite types of music? Are you a hip-hop fan? Perhaps you like jazz or heavy metal or blues or even classical music. If someone asked you to describe your two favorite types of music, what would you choose? If someone asked you what these types of music have in common, what would you say? How would you say they are different?

You compare and contrast items every day. Comparing music types is just one example. Each day you compare one food to another. You compare one article of clothing to another. You even compare teaching styles, books, and school activities. When you make these comparisons, you make a choice. You decide which things you prefer. This process of comparing and contrasting is an important skill in your life. It helps you decide what is important and why. It helps you understand the relationship between one thing and another.

Comparing and contrasting is often used in social studies. When you compare two or more things, you analyze the ways that they are alike. When you contrast two or more things, you analyze the ways that they are different. Ultimately, you use the skill of comparing and contrasting to help you learn more deeply the attributes of a particular idea, object, situation, or person.

In this lesson, you will learn about two types of graphic organizers that are used to show how things are alike and how they are different. The first chart is called a then and now chart. It shows a historical object or idea as it compares to the same type of modern-day item. The second type of organizer is called a Venn diagram. This simple diagram shows clearly what two objects or ideas have in common and how they are different. When you learn how to use these graphic organizers in your reading, you'll discover that text arranged in a compare and contrast organizer is very clear and easy to understand.

Then and Now Charts

Then and now charts compare and contrast events, ideas, situations, or things as they were at a time in the past and as they are today. This type of T-chart helps illustrate what life was like in another time. It points out the changes that have taken place between a time past and today. This can help you see how your life might have been different had you been born at another time. It can also help you realize what types of choices and decisions people faced in the past. Knowing this will help you understand the process of adapting to change—a critical life skill.

When you compare and contrast time periods—or any two or more ideas, objects, or situations—it is important to ask yourself some key questions. These questions will help you focus on what the key points are in your reading and what information you want to gather from the text. The questions are these:

- What do I want to compare and contrast?

- What do I want to learn about the things being compared and contrasted?

- What information do I need to have about both things in order to compare and contrast them?

- What did I learn? What did I discover by comparing and contrasting these things?

Using Then and Now Charts

To create a then and now chart, start with a T-chart. Draw a vertical line in the middle of the page. Next, draw a horizontal line that crosses the vertical line. The chart should look a little like a large letter "t." Write the things you are comparing above the horizontal line, with one on each side of the vertical line. Now write the information about each thing on the appropriate side of the chart. If you have the same type of information about both things—for example, size, color, duration, and so forth—line the information up on both sides of the vertical line. This makes it much easier to see how the things really compare.

Then and Now Charts in Action

On the following page is a letter written by Evelyn, a 95-year-old woman, to her great-great-granddaughter, her namesake, Evie. In it, the older woman describes a few details of what life was like when she was young. After you have read the letter, ask yourself the key questions. Then see how the information has been charted in the then and now chart on page 36. You'll note that there are some entries in the "now" column that don't specifically appear in the letter. That is because the example assumes the reader has some experience or working knowledge of contemporary cars. When you do a then and now chart, you'll often have to fill in information using prior knowledge.

Dear Evie,

Your mother tells me that you will be getting your own car soon! Boy, cars sure are different today than they were in my day. Why, in 1915, when I was really little, I remember the big excitement was that horns went from being the bulb-type that you squeezed to an electric horn that was mounted under the hood. Do you know that all the cars in those days were black? They all looked the same, with gray upholstery. Now you might think that it was hard to tell which car was yours in a parking lot. But guess what? There were no parking lots! That's because only 308,000 cars were built in 1915. Very different from the over 60 million cars that are made each year nowadays! Not everyone owned a car in my day. Mostly it was the folks who had plenty of money. There were still lots of horses and carriages then. And a lot of times the cars scared the horses since they had to share the road. People didn't have garages back then, either. They parked their cars in front of their house or in the barn. They didn't have anything like an SUV or a station wagon or a van in those days. There were only a few different models to choose from—a touring car, a runabout, a sedan, a town car, or a coupe. Whenever we wanted to go on a long trip, we would take the train. Of course, as I got older, our family used the car more and more. But never as much as we use cars today. Can you imagine life without a car, Evie? Anyway, good luck with your new car, and do be careful!

Much love,
your Granny Evelyn

Cars Then and Now

Then: Early Twentieth Century	Now: Early Twenty-First Century
black only color	many different colors
car interiors gray	interiors in many colors
horns hand-blown with air bulbs	electric horns
no parking lots	lots of parking lots
308,000 cars built	60 million cars built
no garages, cars parked on road	most houses have a garage
no SUVs, vans, or station wagons	many models to choose from

Application   Now it's your turn to create a then and now chart. Read the article below about the contrast between women in sports in the Victorian Age and today. Then fill in the then and now chart on page 38.

The Evolution of Women's Sports

If you had been a woman in the Victorian Age, between 1837 and 1901, you probably would not have chosen sports as your number-one interest. In those days, sports were considered masculine and not suitable for delicate females. Women did not participate in sports because of the highly restrictive clothing they wore. To be physically active would mean doing away with corsets, high-topped shoes, long sleeves, and high collars. But women slowly began to ask to join men in some mild athletic interests and pursuits. Slowly, sports were introduced to women—particularly those that included the company of men.

If you were among those first women in sports, you would look very different from the hard-bodied women athletes of today. If you went to college, or if you grew up in a wealthy family, you might be among the first to try some of the newfangled sports, like croquet or archery. These you could play without risking your femininity, and without taking off any of your tight clothes! You might also play golf—again, if you were a rich girl or woman—but you might only play at a country club that had a designated Ladies Day.

If you were like most women interested in sports in Victorian days, tennis might be your game. But don't think you would ever break a sweat. You would play your game on well-manicured lawns, and you would never stretch too hard or exert yourself too much. You would probably play with men as doubles. You would never play against a man, though—what if you were to beat him?

Today, you probably don't think anything of zipping out somewhere on your bike. But if you were a woman in the Victorian Age, riding a bike would be quite revolutionary. For one thing, it would mean that you could go places where you might not be seen, where you might not be safe. And you would have to get rid of your heavy skirts and tight corsets so you could move more freely. You might even wear a crazy pair of bloomers. Bicycling and other sports were responsible for the beginning of the loosening of women's dress codes. Thank goodness!

Today, women can participate in whatever sport they like. They are leaders in running, bodybuilding, even baseball and football. Hard, athletic bodies are considered beautiful and powerful. Women show off their bodies in shorts and sports tops. But women's and men's sports are still not equal. Professional male athletes still make vast sums of money more than their female counterparts if there is even a women's equivalent to compare. Women's sports have yet to be televised in the same way as men's sports. There is still a long way to go. How will sports for women change in your lifetime?

Then and Now Chart

Answer the questions about comparing and contrasting to determine exactly what you are comparing in your then and now chart. What conclusions can you draw based on the information you learned? Complete the then and now chart below. You may need to read between the lines to compare women's sports in the Victorian Age and now.

Women in Sports in the Victorian Age and Today

Then: (Victorian Age: 1837–1901)	Now

Venn Diagrams
One of the most useful graphic tools for comparing and contrasting ideas, people, eras, situations, or events in social studies is the Venn diagram. The diagram was named for a man named John Venn who lived in the mid-1800s. Venn was a historian and an inventor. He invented a machine that could bowl balls automatically. It is said that his machine was so good that it beat a championship bowling team from Australia! He is best remembered for the famous diagram that bears his name. He developed the Venn diagram as a way to illustrate math and logic problems. Today, people use Venn diagrams to compare and contrast many different ideas. It is particularly useful in social studies to compare eras, people, ideas, events, or time periods.

Using Venn Diagrams
The Venn diagram is made by drawing two or more intersecting circles. The parts of the circles that intersect show how the things you are comparing are alike. The parts of the circle that do not intersect show how the things are different.

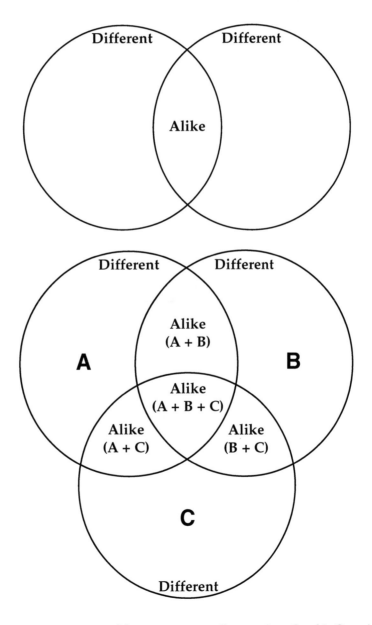

The most important thing to do when you are asked to compare and contrast is to ask yourself three questions: What is being compared? In what ways are the two things different? In what ways are they similar? Once you answer these questions, you can put the answers in the appropriate segments of the Venn circles.

Venn Diagrams in Action

Below is a short article comparing two Native American groups. Notice how they have been charted in the Venn diagram.

Native Americans of the Plains and Woodlands

Before European settlers came to this country, North America was inhabited by many Native American cultures. Each culture had its own way of living, working, and playing. The Plains and the Woodlands cultures had many things in common. Yet there were many differences, too.

The Plains peoples included the Dakota, Cheyenne, Sioux, and Comanche cultures. They lived by using the natural resources around them. The most important resource was the buffalo. They used its meat for food. They used its hide for clothing and shelter. And they used its bones and horns for spoons, cups, toys, and weapons.

Like the Plains peoples, the Woodlands cultures, made up of the Iroquois, Cherokee, and Mound Builders, lived off the natural resources around them. Because they lived in wooded areas, they used wood to make their shelters, called longhouses. Like the Plains cultures, they used animal hides for shelter and clothing. However, unlike the people of the Plains, the Woodlands cultures ate a variety of foods, including fish, berries, fruits, and nuts. They were able to plant crops of corn, beans, and squash.

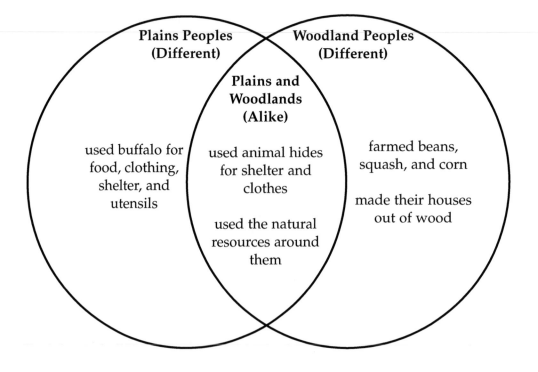

Plains Peoples (Different): used buffalo for food, clothing, shelter, and utensils

Plains and Woodlands (Alike): used animal hides for shelter and clothes; used the natural resources around them

Woodland Peoples (Different): farmed beans, squash, and corn; made their houses out of wood

The article below discusses the two smallest states in the United States. They have much in common, yet in many ways they are quite different. Read the article. Then fill in the Venn diagram on page 42.

The Smallest States

If you've ever traveled around the United States, you know that the states vary in size, shape, climate, landscape, and landform. While it takes more than two days to ride all the way across the state of Texas, it would take less than one hour to ride across Delaware. It would take even less time to ride across Rhode Island.

Delaware and Rhode Island are the nation's smallest states. Delaware is the second smallest, and its little cousin, Rhode Island, ranks first. Delaware is 1,982 square miles, and Rhode Island is just 1,545. And while these little states have much in common, there are many features that differentiate them as well.

Both states were settled originally by Native American cultures. Both were the destinations of early Dutch explorers. Both states are characterized by beautiful coastlines. And both states rely on tourists to boost their state's economy, particularly at their beaches.

Rhode Island and Delaware were both part of the thirteen original states. Delaware proudly boasts being the first state to ratify the U.S. Constitution. Rhode Island was the thirteenth state to ratify the Constitution. Rhode Island was presumably named for the Greek island Rhodes, based on its shape. Delaware was named for the first governor of Virginia, Lord de la Warr.

Rhode Island is part of New England and shares some of the rugged history of shipbuilding and metalworking of New England's heritage. Today, jewelry-making and tourism join this tiny state's thriving industries. Delaware has a dual identity—one town, called Delmar, is divided between Delaware and its neighbor to the south, Maryland (its name is the first three letters of each state name). The Mason-Dixon line is drawn through Delmar, dividing the United States into its official North and South, so important during the Civil War. As a Middle Atlantic state, Delaware has chemical products, food processing, and paper products as its primary industrial manufacturing.

Delaware and Rhode Island are great states to visit. They both have engaging places to see, such as the Winterthur Museum outside Wilmington, Delaware, which features one of the world's best-known naturalistic gardens. Newport, Rhode Island, is also a popular visiting spot. It is historically a shipbuilding town and is known for the elegant mansions built by early twentieth-century millionaires who called Newport their summer home.

If you haven't had a chance to explore the country's smallest states, try it sometime. You'll find that they are both inviting—Delaware will lure you to its sandy Rehoboth Beach on a hot summer afternoon, while Rhode Island will tempt you with its history and its rocky shores.

Venn Diagram Complete the Venn diagram below with information about the ways that Rhode Island and Delaware are different—and alike—as the two smallest states in the nation. Write similarities in the area where the circles intersect. Write differences in the areas where the circles don't intersect. Don't forget to label both circles.

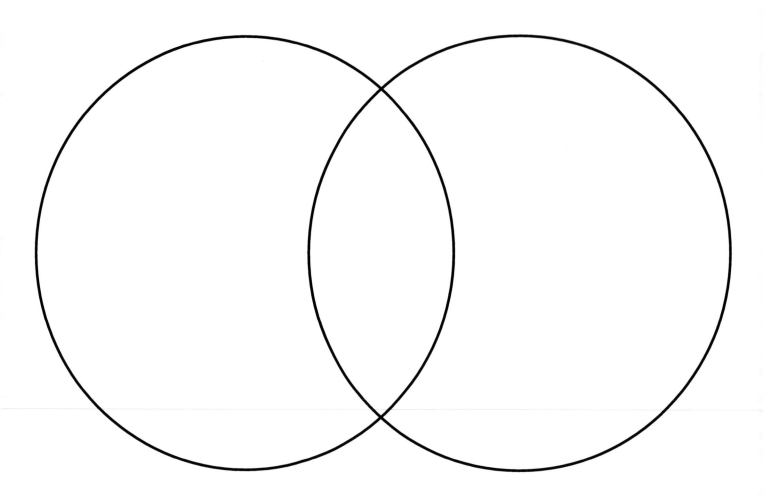

Comparison Matrixes

There are other types of graphic organizers you can use to compare and contrast subjects in social studies. When you are comparing two things that have some similarities, you can use a comparison matrix. This type of graphic organizer is great for comparing things with common elements but different content. For example, if you wanted to use a comparison matrix to compare Delaware and Rhode Island, you might put Delaware in the spot that says "Name 1" and Rhode Island in the spot that says "Name 2." Then you could write attributes both states share at the start of each row. For example, you could include land area, attractions, rank as a state, and chief industries.

	Name 1	Name 2
Attribute 1		
Attribute 2		
Attribute 3		
Attribute 4		
Attribute 5		

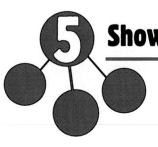

Showing Cause and Effect

Have you ever forgotten to take a book back to the public library? What happened? Did you have to pay a fine? Have you ever left the milk out of the fridge? Chances are it went bad, and you couldn't drink it.

The examples above describe events and the reasons they happened. *If* you forget to bring your book back to the library, *then* you pay a fine. *If* you leave the milk out of the fridge, *then* you can't use it because it has spoiled. This if . . . then link represents a relationship known as cause and effect. The effect is the thing that happens. The cause is the thing that makes it happen. Here's how it works with the above examples:

Cause ———————————————▶ **Effect**

forget to take books back to library   must pay fine
leave milk out of fridge   milk spoils

In social studies, cause and effect relationships are a way to understand why things happened and what made them happen. So often a turn of events triggers other really important events, such as the assassination of Archduke Ferdinand of Austria, which signaled the start of World War I.

Causes and effects aren't always easy to spot when you're reading a text. That requires some critical-thinking skills. But it is important to recognize causes and effects, because they can help you make better decisions, understand consequences and outcomes, and solve problems. They can also help you analyze information and events so that you can determine the accuracy of what you're reading or what you're listening to. Luckily, there are some techniques you can use to recognize a cause and effect pattern. One of the most important techniques is to ask yourself these questions:

- What caused this event or situation to happen? (What is the cause?)

- What are the consequences of this event or situation? (What is the effect?)

It is also important to remember that some events have a number of causes or consequences. You'll also discover that cause and effect are not necessarily laid out clearly in a historic document or text. Sometimes the effect will be stated first. Sometimes you will need to infer the cause based on the events or facts presented. Sometimes you will have to use prior knowledge to draw a conclusion about the effect of an event.

Cause and Effect Maps

A cause-and-effect map is a graphic organizer that can help you analyze why an event took place and what the consequences of that event were. One way to recognize that a cause and effect pattern is being used is to look for key words and phrases in the text. These words signal that a cause and effect pattern is being used.

Cause	Effect
because	as a result
due to	therefore
since	resulted in
as a result of	thus
if	as a consequence
began	caused
	led to
	so
	then

Using Cause and Effect Maps

To make a cause and effect map, you must first determine if your text involves one cause leading to one effect, or more complex cause and effect relationships. For example, you might find one cause leading to several effects, or one effect with several causes. The basic approach to organizing causes and effects is the same for each situation—you write the cause on the left and the effect on the right, with an arrow going from the cause to the effect—but the specific arrangement varies.

If you have one cause for each effect, the organizer can be very simple. For each cause, draw an oval on the left side of the page. Write the cause in the oval. On the right side of the page, draw a rectangle for each effect. Write the effect in the rectangle. Draw an arrow from each oval to each rectangle.

Of course, in social studies, many events have more than one cause, or more than one effect. If you have one cause leading to several effects, draw a large rectangle on the left side of the page. Write the cause in that box. On the right side of the page, draw a smaller rectangle for each effect. Write one effect in each box. Draw arrows from the cause box to each effect box.

If you have many causes leading to one effect, draw a rectangle on the left side of the page for each cause. Write the causes in the boxes. Draw a rectangle on the right side of the page for the effect. Write the effect in the box. Draw arrows from the cause boxes to the effect box.

Cause and Effect Maps in Action

Read the story that follows about Raimi Rowan, who forgot to gas up his car the night before an important exam. See how many causes and effects you can find. Then check out the charts below and on page 47 to see if you found them all.

Raimi's Regret

It was the big day. The last exam ever in college. The last test before medical school. The last day in college before Raimi began his journey to discover the cure for the common cold. The most important day ever. If he didn't do well on this exam, he would lose everything.

He woke with a start—he had overslept. No matter—he would skip breakfast. All that mattered was that he get to the exam on time.

He dressed quickly, got to his car, and began his short drive to the college. He looked at the gas gauge. Darn! He had meant to put some gas in last night. Oh well, he'd get there. It wasn't too far. Just as he turned the first corner, the car began to stall. He wasn't going to make it. He pulled the car to the side of the road. Please let someone come by, please, please! Five minutes went by, then ten. He was too impatient to just wait there. So he started for the gas station four blocks away. By now it was 8:10. The exam had begun. He knew he wasn't going to make it. His dream was shattered. There were no make-up exams. This had been his only chance. Now the world would have to wait for someone else to discover the cure for the common cold.

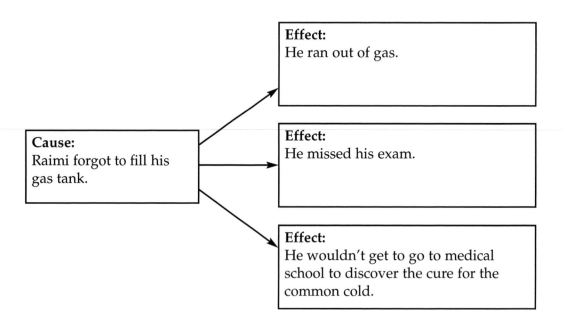

Cause:
Raimi forgot to fill his gas tank.

Effect:
He ran out of gas.

Effect:
He missed his exam.

Effect:
He wouldn't get to go to medical school to discover the cure for the common cold.

46

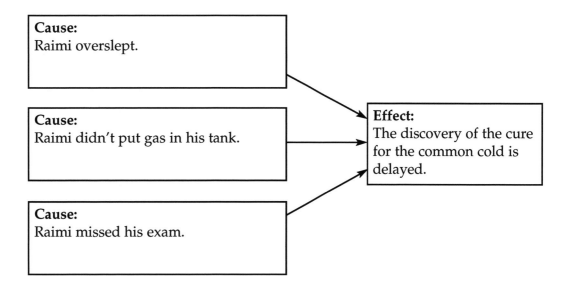

Cause:
Raimi overslept.

Cause:
Raimi didn't put gas in his tank.

Cause:
Raimi missed his exam.

Effect:
The discovery of the cure for the common cold is delayed.

Application Now it's your turn. Create a cause and effect map based on the text below. Be sure to ask yourself these questions:

• What caused this event or situation to happen? (What is the cause?)

• What are the consequences of this event or situation? (What is the effect?)

Accidental Invention

Bette Nesmith Graham had always dreamed of being an artist. But when she found herself divorced and a single mother of a young boy, she knew that she had to put her dreams of being an artist on hold. She took some classes and learned to be a wonderful executive secretary, proud of her work each day.

Even though she had put her art on hold, she still enjoyed dabbling in her rare free time. One day when she was thinking about her work and how to make it more efficient, she wondered what would happen if she could correct tiny mistakes on her typewritten work without having to type her letters and memos over again. She worked in her kitchen, and combining some tempera paint in her blender, she whipped up a liquid to paint over her typos. If artists could cover their work with paint, why couldn't secretaries?

Graham put her paint in a tiny bottle, attached a watercolor brush to it, and brought it to work. Luckily, her boss never noticed her few typos. Soon other secretaries wanted some of her Mistake Out, as she called it. By 1956, she had begun a miniature lab in her kitchen and was filling orders for friends in the business. She wasn't making much money—there was not enough time to make big batches to sell—until she got fired from her job. Then she began her work as an entrepreneur in earnest. By 1967, Graham had a million-dollar company. Less than ten years later, Liquid Paper was headquartered in a huge warehouse in

Dallas, Texas, with 500 bottles of her invention manufactured every minute.

Graham always remembered her roots as a single mother. Even when she grew very rich, she used her money to fund foundations to help women make a living. Just before she died, she sold her company for $47.5 million. Today, Liquid Paper is a staple in every desk drawer—even the delete key on computers hasn't put it out of business!

Cause and Effect Map

Use the information in the reading to fill out the cause and effect map below. Start by asking what the event is and what the consequences of the event are. You may also think of more than one effect in this story. Once you've decided the effects (or events), you'll be able to determine the causes.

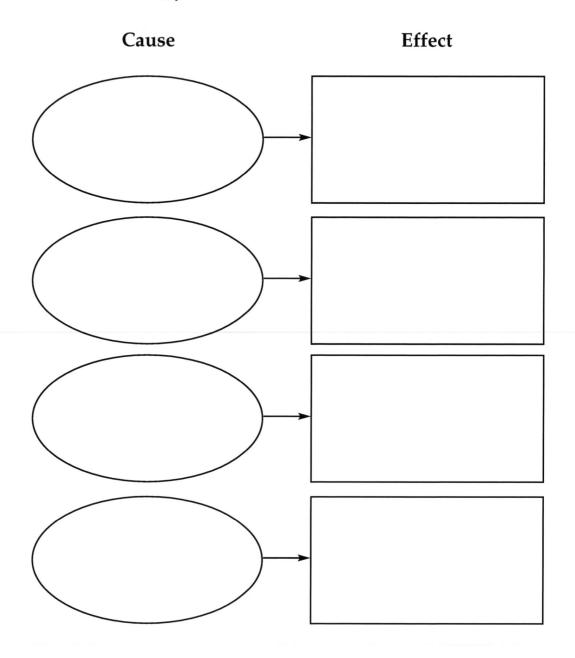

Cause	Effect

Problem/Solution Charts

Are you a good problem solver? It takes special skills to be good at solving a problem. One of the most important skills is learning how to see what the problem is in the first place. It's easy to get overwhelmed by the details and not see the real problem.

One of life's goals is to meet challenges, figure out how to solve them, and grow stronger. In history, problems and challenges are what we study. One interesting aspect of history is seeing how people choose to solve the challenges they face. Once we understand how people solve problems, we can become better at it ourselves. That's one of the greatest advantages of studying history and social studies!

Using Problem/Solution Charts

When reading social studies or history texts, it is often helpful to identify what problem or challenge is being addressed. Then it is important to analyze the action people take to solve the problem. Finally, you can then see the result, or what happens as a result of the action. This process of identifying the problem can be done by asking these questions:

- What is the problem or challenge that people want to address?

- What action do people take to try to address the challenging or problematic situation?

- What happens as a result of the action?

You can organize this information graphically by using a problem/solution chart. This type of organizer is a cousin to the cause and effect organizer, since solving a problem requires knowing what the cause and effect of an issue or an event really are.

Problem/Solution Charts in Action

Read the following article about the *Apollo 13* mission to the Moon in 1970. As you read, stop and think about what the problem is. Then take a moment to predict what you think the action to solve the problem should be. Read to find out what people did to solve the problem and what happened as a result. Then see how this information is shown on the problem/solution chart below.

The Successful Failure

For eight long days in April of 1970, three astronauts—Jim Lovell, Fred Haise, and Jack Swigert—were kept alive by the extraordinary teamwork of a group of people who couldn't even see them from the ground.

Apollo 13 was thought of as a fairly routine Moon flight. The crewmembers were to collect rocks from the Fra Mauro region of the Moon. But fifty-five hours into the flight, a failure occurred in the service module oxygen system. This meant that there was not enough oxygen, water, or power to continue the mission to the Moon. Instead, the astronauts were lucky to live through their mission at all.

What saved them was the ingenuity of the people who worked in Houston, Texas, the home base for the lunar project. The members of the large land crew were forced to think as if they were the astronauts themselves. What would they do to save power? The crew stayed up overnight, never leaving the Houston Control area, in order to think creatively about how to help the *Apollo 13* crew stay alive. Luckily their efforts paid off. They figured out a makeshift solution to keep the energy and oxygen from draining out of the astronauts' small module. However, there have been no trips to the Moon since the *Apollo 13* near disaster.

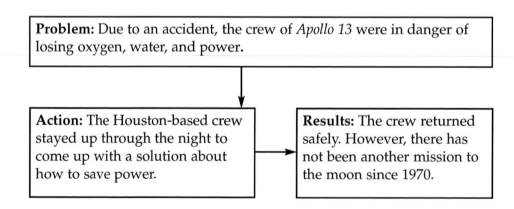

Problem: Due to an accident, the crew of *Apollo 13* were in danger of losing oxygen, water, and power.

Action: The Houston-based crew stayed up through the night to come up with a solution about how to save power.

Results: The crew returned safely. However, there has not been another mission to the moon since 1970.

Application Now it's your turn to identify a problem and the ways the problem is solved. Read the article below about the difficult election night in 2000, when there was no clear winner of the presidential election. As you read, think about what the problem really is, and what the solution should be. Then fill out the problem/solution chart on page 52.

The Long Night

Most election nights are long, but none was longer than the one that took place on November 6, 2000. That night, there was no official winner of the election.

On November 6, most voting areas had reported their votes. The race between then Vice President Al Gore and Texas Governor George W. Bush was tighter than any election in the recent past. Late Election night, news organizations predicted Gore would win. Later still, they withdrew their predictions for Gore and said that Bush would win. By 5:00 A.M., they withdrew that prediction as well. There was no clear winner.

Why was it so hard to tell who was the winner? One of the key issues in the election was the confusing ballots and defective voting machines that were used in Florida. People there voted by punching a voting card and creating a hole next to the name of the person they wanted to elect. The little piece of paper that is punched out of the voting card is called a chad. If the punch isn't complete, then it is hard to tell whom the voter really wanted for president.

People still disagree about who really won the election. The decision went to the Florida Supreme Court and then to the U.S. Supreme Court. But not everyone agreed with the courts' decisions. Bush was declared the winner by just 537 votes. Those who favored Gore were bitterly disappointed. Those who favored Bush were thrilled. Today, the election process in Florida has been improved with new electronic voting and better vote counting. No one wants to see a repeat of election night 2000.

Problem/Solution Chart

Use the reading on page 51 to fill in the problem/solution chart below. Write the problem in the top box. Write the action taken to address the problem in the "Action" box. Write the results of the action taken in the "Results" box.

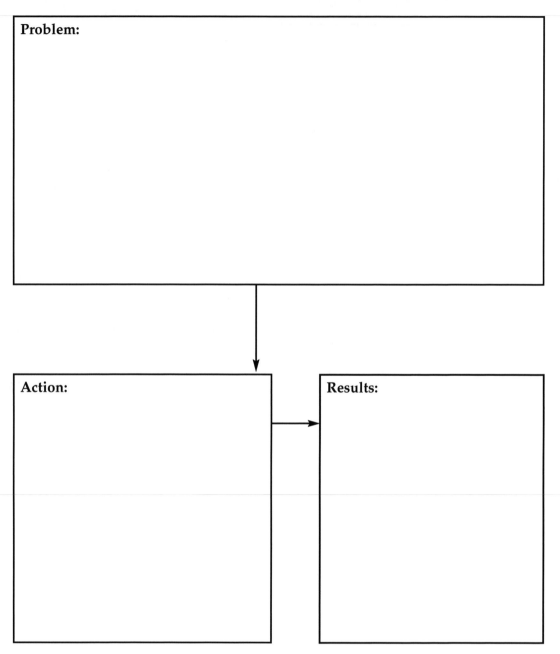

Problem:

Action:

Results:

Event Maps Another way to determine cause and effect is by mapping out the events that make up a historic time period. An event map is a very useful tool that shows what the concept or event is and what made it happen, why, how, where, when, and who. See if you can use the event map below to chart the events of the 2000 election or of the *Apollo 13* space mission.

Write the event in the circle. Write a few words or a phrase in each box to show what happened, when it happened, where it happened, how it happened, why it happened, and who was involved.

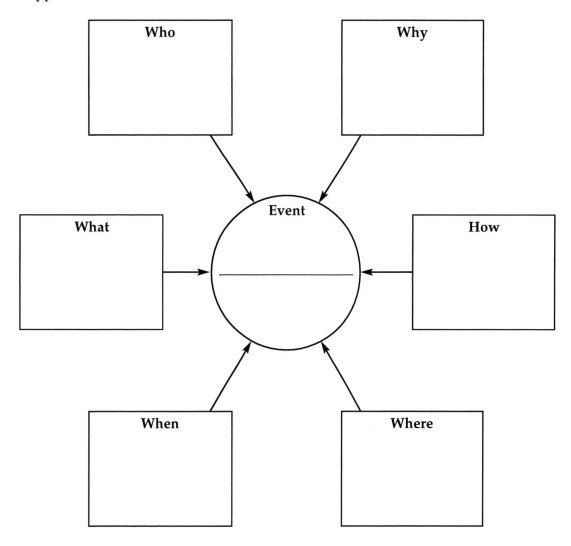

6 Writing

As you have learned, graphic organizers are very helpful when you are reading. They are also helpful when you are writing. In this lesson, you'll learn about using graphic organizers as you write history or social studies assignments. More often than not, writing for social studies classes involves both research and analysis. Graphic organizers can help you get your thoughts together, gather your notes, and present your information clearly in writing. Once you know how to use these writing tools, you'll find that you can use them over and over again in your social studies classes.

Graphic organizers are a great tool to use as you plan your writing. Most of your writing is probably done using the writing process. The writing process helps writers organize their thoughts. It also helps writers avoid frustration and use their time efficiently. There are four basic steps in the writing process: prewriting, writing, revising, and publication. In this lesson, we will look at graphic organizers that you can use for the first two steps, prewriting and writing.

We will use a model question to show how you can use graphic organizers to write about social studies. Here is the model question:

  • Choose an explorer from the twentieth century. Write about his or her exploration and how the exploration made an impact on society.

Now choose a topic that interests you from the list on page 55 and practice using each graphic organizer with the topic you chose.

Social Studies Research Topics

1. The Civil War changed the lives of African Americans in the United States. In what ways were their lives affected?

2. Geography plays an important role in the character of a region. Choose two world regions. Compare and contrast the geography of both regions. Discuss the ways that geography affects the type of work and culture found in each area.

3. During the nineteenth century, wars were fought in many parts of the world. They included revolutions, wars of conquest, and civil wars. Choose one war from this period. Discuss the causes, combatants, and consequences of this war.

4. Research the difference between a democracy and a republic. Find out why the framers of the U.S. Constitution chose to make the United States a republic rather than a democracy.

5. What do you think might have happened if the U.S. Constitution had been written this year instead of over 200 years ago? In what ways would the document be different? How would it reflect the needs of our current society?

6. What were the events that led up to the 1955 bus boycott in Montgomery, Alabama? What happened as a result of the boycott?

7. Trace the evolution of women's clothing in the twentieth century. In what ways do changes in women's fashion reflect the changing roles of women during that period?

8. Trace the history of your state or territory. What people and events had the most influence in shaping this history?

9. Interview an older family member or friend. Find out what inventions were new when he or she was the age you are today. In what ways did these inventions affect society?

10. Think about some important events that have taken place since you were born. In terms of world history, what single event do you consider the most important? Describe the event. Then give reasons for your choice.

Prewriting   The first part of the writing process is prewriting. This is the work you do before you actually begin to write. It is the most important part of your writing. Once the prewriting stage is done, you'll have done most of the planning for your work. The only thing left will be to put the sentences to paper. That part will be easy because you will already have organized everything you want to say!

The prewriting stage includes several different tasks. You need to choose a topic, narrow it, establish a purpose for writing, research the topic, and plan your writing by creating an outline. For the purposes of this lesson, either you have already chosen a topic from the list on page 55, or you are using the model question. So we will start with narrowing the topic.

Narrowing the Topic   Writing topics are often very broad. The first step in prewriting is narrowing the topic. Start by identifying several subtopics that fit the requirements of the question. Then decide which of them you find most interesting. Using the model question, you might use your prior knowledge to identify areas of exploration in the twentieth century. Your experience tells you that there were several areas, including:

- space

- Antarctica

- the oceans

- the North Pole

- rain forests

- the Himalayan region

Let's say that you choose Antarctica. Now that you have an area of exploration, you need to choose an explorer. If you already know a bit about Antarctica, you may be able to do this right away. If not, you may need to do a little reading first. Let's say that you decide to write about Sir Ernest Shackleton's 1914–1916 Antarctic expedition. You have successfully taken a broad topic—twentieth-century explorers—and narrowed it to a manageable topic.

Defining a Purpose for Writing

Once you've chosen a writing topic, the next step is to define your purpose for writing. The purpose is what you are trying to achieve by writing. Are you trying to explain how something happened, or trying to present information about a topic? Do you want to describe something? Perhaps you want to analyze an event, with the causes that led up to it and the consequences of the event. You might want to persuade someone to do something, or convince them that an idea or a theory is correct. You might just want to express an idea or an opinion. Each of these purposes will affect the way you write your essay. It's possible that you will include elements of more than one purpose. But it is important to decide your main approach. In social studies, most essays have one of the following purposes:

- to inform or explain

- to describe

- to analyze

- to persuade

- to express thoughts or opinions

Look back at your narrowed topic. Why are you writing about this topic? For the Shackleton paper, imagine that you have decided to describe the expedition. This means that you will describe the people, places, and events of the trip. You will also use analysis to decide how the trip made an impact on society.

KWL Charts   Before you begin researching your topic, you should figure out what you already know about your topic and what you still need to find out before you can write an effective paper. One helpful tool for this part of the process is the KWL chart. A KWL chart has spaces for what you KNOW, what you WANT to know, and what you LEARNED. It is a great way to get started on research.

Using KWL Charts   The first step in using a KWL chart is to see what you already know about the topic. You may want to decide what drew you to the topic to begin with. In the **K** part of the chart, you write all the information you already know.

In the **W** part of the chart, you write any questions that you have about your topic. Think about what your readers might want to know, as well as your purpose for writing.

Then, once you've done some preliminary research, you can write down what you've learned in the **L** part of the chart. This shouldn't include all the details; it should be just a general overview of new things you learn about your topic. You'll be writing more detailed notes later on. Don't forget to write your topic at the top of the chart.

KWL Charts in Action   Let's look at the Shackleton model. Here's a sample KWL chart for this topic:

Topic: Shackleton Expedition

K	W	L
Shackleton was from England and explored in the early 1900s.	What made Shackleton want to explore Antarctica?	The expedition took place in 1914. This was not Shackleton's first voyage. He had been part of earlier expeditions.
He and his crew wanted to explore Antarctica.	Who was Shackleton's crew?	Shackleton could not be the first to explore Antarctica, but he wanted to be the first to cross the continent. Twenty-seven men answered a newspaper ad Shackleton placed.
They were trapped for a really long time.	What happened to the expedition?	Their ship was crushed by the ice; they spent months camping on the ice, then made it to a small, barren island Shackleton's leadership, optimism kept crew going.
Eventually, the crew was rescued.	How did the crew survive? How were they rescued?	Shackleton left crew on Elephant island, went 800 miles in open water to South Georgia, reached whaling station. Then Shackleton went back to Elephant Island and rescued crew. Everyone lived.

Application Use the blank KWL chart below to chart the information you know, would like to know, and have learned about the topic you have chosen.

Topic: _____

K What I KNOW	W What I WANT to Know	L What I LEARNED

Note-Taking Organizers

The next prewriting step is collecting information about the topic. This usually calls for some research. Most people choose to do research by using reliable Internet sites and library books on the topic, taking accurate notes as they find new information.

Remember, taking notes does not mean copying information word for word. The key to good note-taking is to write down only key facts, with a clear reference to the source of the information. Copying whole sentences can make it hard to remember which material comes from another source and which is your own. Using someone else's words is plagiarism. Whether it is done intentionally or by mistake, plagiarism in a paper will result in a failing grade. You can easily avoid problems with research by keeping careful track of your sources and by jotting down key phrases and words rather than whole sentences.

There are several good ways to keep track of notes. One approach is to use 3×5 cards and keep one fact on each card. Another way is to use a graphic organizer like the one on the next page. This organizer has a space for everything you need to keep track of.

Using Note-Taking Organizers

This organizer has a section for each information source you use. Start by writing down information about the source. If it is a book, write down the title of the book, the name of the author, and any other details your teacher requires for a bibliography, such as the year of publication and the name of the publisher. If the source is a web page, write down the name of the page, the page's author, if available, and the URL for the page. For each source, use the other boxes in that section to note important information. For each note, write down the number of the page where you found the information. Then write a few brief phrases to capture the information. Don't copy word for word!

Note-Taking Organizers in Action

This is what a note-taking organizer for the paper on Shackleton might look like:

Research Topic: Ernest Shackleton and the *Endurance* expedition			
Research Source 1 Author: Lansing, Alfred Title: *Endurance*	Note: p. 12 S. bought ship called *Polaris,* renamed it *Endurance* after family motto: "By endurance we conquer."	Note: p. 12 5,000 people volunteered to be part of the expedition.	Note: p. 12-13 S. picked 27 men in all. Some were people he had sailed with before. Others he picked by intuition. For example, asked Dr. Alexander Macklin if he could sing.
Research Source 2 Author: Rubin, Jeff Title: *Encyclopedia Encarta Internet* http://encarta.msn.com /text_761558323/Shac kleton_Sir_Ernest_He nry.html	Note: intro: S. was born 1874, died 1922	Note: First expeditions: S. had tried a few expeditions earlier, including one with Robert Falcon Scott. S. got sick, then went again in 1907.	Note: First expeditions: S. was knighted in 1909 for setting the record for the farthest southern latitude reached.
Research Source 3 Author: Khan, Adam Title: *All in Your Head* www.youmeworks.com	Note: p. 2 *Endurance* trapped in ice. Crew spent 10 months waiting for ice to break up. Took lifeboats from *Endurance,* dragged them 9 miles over ice, sailed to lifeless Elephant Island.	Note: p. 3 S. took 5 crewmen from Elephant Island over long passage to St. George's.	Note: p. 4 S., 2 crewmen climbed over steep mountains on St. George's. No one had crossed them before. Survived; arrived at whaling station in tattered clothes. Then went back to Elephant Island to rescue rest of crew.

Application Use the graphic organizer below to take research notes for your topic. Add and delete boxes as needed. Remember to write down the source and use brief phrases. Don't copy word for word!

Research Topic:			
Research Source 1 Author: Title:	Note: p. _____	Note: p. _____	Note: p. _____
Research Source 2 Author: Title:	Note: p. _____	Note: p. _____	Note: p. _____
Research Source 3 Author: Title:	Note: p. _____	Note: p. _____	Note: p. _____

Outlines   The next step in the prewriting process is planning. This is where you decide what you want to include in your writing and what you can leave out. This is also where you decide what supporting details to include. You can use an outline to help your planning.

An outline is an organized overview of an essay, written in short phrases. It is a type of map or scheme that shows the way your writing will progress logically. The purpose of an outline is to organize your information. Outlines help you determine the beginning, middle, and end of your work. They can show how your ideas are related to one another.

Outlines can be either informal or formal. We'll look at a formal outline first.

Formal Outlines   A formal outline is often used in informational or expository writing. Formal outlines don't include complete sentences or punctuation. Each line includes just a few important words or a key phrase. Later on, you will turn these into topic sentences and supporting details for the paragraphs of your essay.

A formal outline follows a very specific pattern. The most important information is written along the left of the page. Less important information is indented—set in—from the left. The farther from the left of the page a piece of information is, the less important it is.

The most important pieces of information are the main points you want to make or topics you want to cover. They are labeled with Roman numerals. Subtopics under each topic are indented and labeled with capital letters. Details that support the subtopics are indented even more and labeled with regular (Arabic) numerals. If you need to add another level of detail, you can indent again, using lowercase letters to identify these details. Once the outline is complete, you can tell at a glance which information is most important.

Using Formal Outlines   Begin your outline by writing the title of your paper at the top of the page. Next, identify the main topics you want to address or points you want to make in your paper. Write the Roman numeral I on the left side of the page. Write your most important topic or point next to the I. This is usually something that will introduce the essay and explain what you are trying to say, such as your thesis statement.

Now, identify any subtopics in this main topic, or ideas that clarify the main point. Under the first main point, indented a little from the left, write a capital letter A. Write a subtopic or a piece of information that supports your point next to the letter A. Do the same thing for any other facts that support this point, using a different capital letter for each.

Next, identify any details or examples that develop your supporting ideas. Under the first subtopic, indented a little more from the left, write an Arabic numeral 1. Write a detail or an example next to the numeral. Do the same thing for any other details or examples that develop this point, using a different numeral for each.

Continue with the same pattern for your other main topics, using Roman numerals for the main topics, capital letters for subtopics, and Arabic numerals for details and examples. The last main point should offer a conclusion to the rest of the points. It often includes a restatement of the main idea. When you finish, you will have the basic structure for your essay.

A formal outline pattern looks like this:

Title

I. Introduction

    A. Opening statement

    B. Main idea or thesis

II. First major idea or topic

    A. Subtopic or clarifying idea

        1. Detail or example

        2. Detail or example

    B. Subtopic or clarifying idea

        1. Detail or example

        2. Detail or example

III. Second major idea or topic

    A. Subtopic or clarifying idea

        1. Detail or example

        2. Detail or example

    B. Subtopic or clarifying idea

        1. Detail or example

        2. Detail or example

IV. Conclusion

    A. Restatement of main idea

    B. Final statement

The number of Roman numerals, letters, and Arabic numerals depends on how many topics and subtopics you include in your paper.

Formal Outlines in Action

Now let's see what the outline for a research paper on the Shackleton voyage might look like.

Sir Ernest Shackleton and the Voyage of the *Endurance*

I. Introduction
    A. Voyage of the *Endurance* one of the greatest explorations of the twentieth century
    B. Crew survived because of determination, optimism, endurance

II. Background
    A. Shackleton arranged funding to explore, cross Antarctica
    B. Gathered crew
        1. Advertised for crew
        2. Describe some crew members
    C. Set sail August 1914

III. What happened after *Endurance* reached Weddell Sea
    A. Ship trapped in ice
        1. What crew did to keep alive and active before ship broke up
        2. What crew did after ship broke up to stay alive on ice floe
    B. Ice floe broke up
        1. Trip to Elephant Island
        2. Staying alive on Elephant Island

IV. Rescue
    A. Shackleton, 5 crew members set off in small boat
        1. Sailed 800 miles to St. George's Island
        2. Forced by storm to land on wrong side of island
        3. Climbed treacherous mountains to reach whaling station
    B. Shackleton made three attempts to set sail from St. George's Island, rescue other crew members
        1. Finally able to set off four and a half months after leaving crew
        2. Found all crew members alive; all expedition members survived

V. Conclusion
    A. Voyage of *Endurance*, crew story of amazing stamina, leadership
        1. Ten areas around Antarctica named after Shackleton
        2. Shackleton's leadership style still studied today for lessons to apply to other situations

Application Now it's your turn. Use the blank outline below to create an outline based on the notes you've taken for your research project. Remember to use short phrases that you can later turn into topic sentences for each paragraph of your paper. Add or delete lines as needed.

Title _____

I. Introduction

    A. Opening statement _____

           _____

    B. Main idea or thesis _____

II. First major idea or topic _____

    A. Subtopic or clarifying idea _____

        1. Detail or example _____

        2. Detail or example _____

    B. Subtopic or clarifying idea _____

        1. Detail or example _____

        2. Detail or example _____

III. Second major idea or topic _____

    A. Subtopic or clarifying idea _____

        1. Detail or example _____

        2. Detail or example _____

    B. Subtopic or clarifying idea _____

        1. Detail or example _____

        2. Detail or example _____

IV. Conclusion _____

    A. Restatement of main idea _____

    B. Final statement _____

Informal Outlines

An informal outline is very similar to a formal outline. Like a formal outline, it gives an overview of the way the paper will be developed. Unlike a formal outline, it does not use a system of Roman numerals, capital letters, and Arabic numerals. An informal outline may use short phrases, or it may use complete sentences for the main topics and supporting points. It includes an indication of how each supporting point will be developed, such as by using examples, descriptions, comparisons, and so forth. An informal outline often begins with a thesis statement—a statement of what the essay is designed to show.

Using Informal Outlines

Informal outlines are a good way of organizing information when a formal outline is not really required. Because informal outlines often include complete sentences, it is easy to move from the outline to a first draft of the essay. These outlines can be especially useful in an exam setting, where you don't have the time or resources for a formal outline.

Informal Outlines in Action

Here is an example of an informal outline for an essay about the voyage of the *Endurance*.

Topic: Sir Ernest Shackleton and the Voyage of the *Endurance*

> **Thesis statement:** The voyage of the *Endurance* was one of the greatest explorations of the twentieth century. The crew survived because of a mixture of determination, optimism, and endurance—and the leadership skills of Sir Ernest Shackleton.

> **Support Statement 1:** Sir Ernest Shackleton was already an experienced explorer when he put the expedition together.
> **Developed by:** description of Shackleton's experience, how he set up the expedition, hired crew, etc. Quote: "help wanted" ad.

> **Support Statement 2:** All went well until after the expedition left South Georgia Island, heading for the Weddell Sea. By January 19, the *Endurance* was solidly frozen in pack ice, and the struggle to survive began.
> **Developed by:** description of what crew did to survive in blizzards, below-zero temperatures of Antarctic winter, preparations they made for possibility of ship being crushed by ice

> **Support Statement 3:** On October 23, after 281 days locked in the ice, the *Endurance* was crushed by the pressure, and the next phase of the ordeal began as the crewmen used open boats to try to reach land.
> **Developed by:** description of setting up camp on the ice, dragging boats miles to reach open water, optimism despite desperate situation; quote from S.: "After long months of ceaseless anxiety and strain . . . we have been compelled to abandon the ship, which is crushed beyond all hope of ever being righted, we are alive and well, and we have stores and equipment for the task that lies before us. The task is to reach land with all the members of the Expedition"; description of trip to barren Elephant Island; detail: first time they touched land in 16 months

Support Statement 4: Despite all the hardship the men had already endured, the next part of the ordeal was the hardest yet. With a crew of five men, Shackleton set off in an open boat to cross 800 miles of the most storm-swept water in the world to get help for his crew.

Developed by: description of preparing boat, choosing crew, navigating with no visibility, chipping ice off boat to keep weight from sinking them, arrival on wrong side of St. George's Island; trek over island to reach whaling station, abortive attempts to return to Elephant Island, final departure after four months, rescue of remaining crew members; all survived; quote Shackleton's query to Wild, Wild's response: "Are you all well?" "All safe, all well!"

Conclusion: The voyage of the *Endurance* and her crew is a story of amazing stamina and leadership skills, as without Shackleton, the men would probably not have survived.

Developed by: other expeditions where many men were lost, although conditions were not as hard; S.'s choice of Wild to keep group together on island; how he kept Worsley, Crean going on trek over St. George's Island; leadership style still studied today for lessons to apply to other situations

Application Try organizing your notes into the informal outline below. Say how you will develop each supporting point. Possible approaches include example, comparison, contrast, definition, description, narrative, quotations, and paraphrases of research material. Add or delete boxes as needed.

Topic:

Thesis statement:

Support Statement 1: Developed by:

Support Statement 2: Developed by:

Support Statement 3: Developed by:

Support Statement 4: Developed by:

Conclusion: Developed by:

Expository Writing Organizers

Once you've done all the prewriting, it's time to actually start writing. Graphic organizers can help you here, too. For the writing stage, you can use a writing organizer. This will create the skeleton of the sentences you want to include. This is a place where you can begin to do some preliminary editing and culling out of unnecessary information.

Using Expository Writing Organizers

An expository writing organizer is a great way to lay out most of your work before you begin writing. Like an outline, an expository writing organizer can be formal or informal. The formal organizer breaks your paragraphs into headings, much like the outline. However, the expository writing organizer includes full sentences that you can transfer directly into your writing, as well as transition words or phrases to connect paragraphs and ideas. Once you have completed this part of the process, you should have a first draft of your paper.

To complete the expository writing organizer, start by writing the title of your essay at the top. In the first box, write the opening sentences of your paper. This should include your thesis statement—a sentence that tells your readers what the essay will be about and what point you will be making.

In the next box, write a transition word, phrase, or sentence to link your introduction with the first paragraph of the body of the essay. In the next box, write the topic sentence for the first body paragraph. Then add sentences for the supporting details. Complete the rest of the organizer, following the same pattern: topic sentence, details, transition.

Expository Writing Organizers in Action

Here is an expository writing organizer for the essay on the *Endurance*:

Topic: Sir Ernest Shackleton and the Voyage of the *Endurance*

Opening Sentences: Sir Ernest Shackleton and his crew led one of the greatest explorations of the twentieth century. Their success was based on determination, optimism, and endurance.

Transition: Were it not for Shackleton's great leadership, the voyage of the *Endurance* could have ended tragically.

Paragraph 1 Topic sentence: Preparing for the expedition was challenging.
Supporting details: With the outbreak of the First World War, many people were unwilling to give money for exploration.
Shackleton finally was able to gather the funds he needed.
Then he went about choosing his crew.
Over 5,000 men volunteered for the voyage. Most of them were people who loved the sense of adventure and exploration. Shackleton chose mostly veteran seamen for the core of his crew.
For the remaining crew, Shackleton made quick decisions based on how the men looked and if they had a sense of humor as well as discipline.
It might have seemed that Shackleton didn't put much thought into choosing the crew, but he had a great ability to build a team he could trust and who would trust him.

Transition: The voyage set sail in August 1914.

Paragraph 2 Topic sentence: In January 1915, the *Endurance* was trapped in the ice of the Weddell Sea.
Supporting details: The ship remained fixed in the ice until the ship was finally crushed and sank.
The crew rescued three small boats that they would later use to make their way to Elephant Island.
In freezing cold and blizzards, the crew dragged the heavy boats over uneven ice that often broke apart as they crossed.
Through it all, they remained optimistic that they would survive. Shackleton's leadership kept them upbeat and hopeful.

Transition: The ice finally opened up enough for the crew to put the boats in the water. They landed on desolate Elephant Island, but without supplies, they couldn't survive there for long.

Paragraph 3 Topic sentence: Shackleton and five of his crew set off to St. George's Island for help.
Supporting details: The 800-mile trip from Elephant Island to St. George's involved crossing the most storm-swept waters in the world and navigating without being able to see the sun.
After seventeen grueling days the crew landed at St. George's, only to discover that they had landed on the wrong side of the island.
Shackleton and two other crewmen set off to trek over the mountains to the whaling station. No one had ever succeeded in crossing the island before.
They climbed without stopping for thirty-six hours. The last part of the climb was spent sliding down the ice-covered slope.
When they reached safety, Shackleton immediate set about finding a way to rescue his remaining men.

Transition: For Shackleton, the most important goal was to rescue the crew.

Conclusion: Shackleton succeeded in rescuing his crew. Even though he didn't achieve his goal of crossing Antarctica, his voyage was considered a success because he and his crew survived such terrible conditions. Today, Shackleton's leadership style is still studied to determine what it is he did to keep his crew alive.

Application Now it's your turn. Use your outline to fill in the expository writing organizer below. Add or delete sections as needed.

Opening Sentences:

Transition: .

Paragraph 1 Topic sentence:

Supporting details:

Transition:

Paragraph 2 Topic sentence:

Supporting details:

Transition:

Paragraph 3 Topic sentence:

Supporting details:

Transition:

Conclusion:

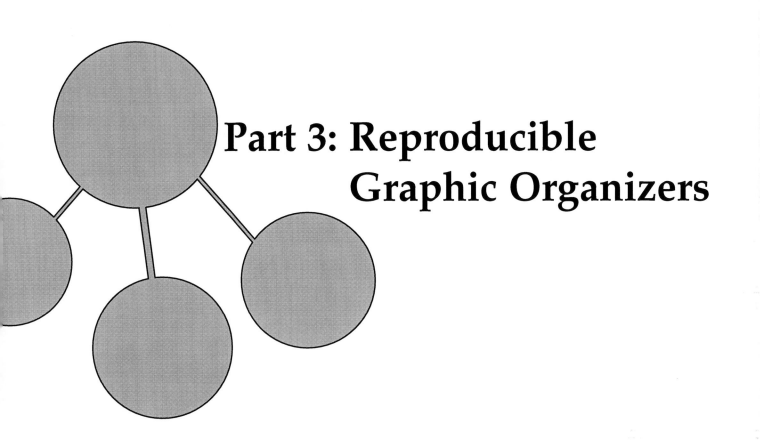

Part 3: Reproducible Graphic Organizers

Concept/Event Map

Write your topic in the center circle. Then write details in the smaller circles. Add and delete lines and circles as needed.

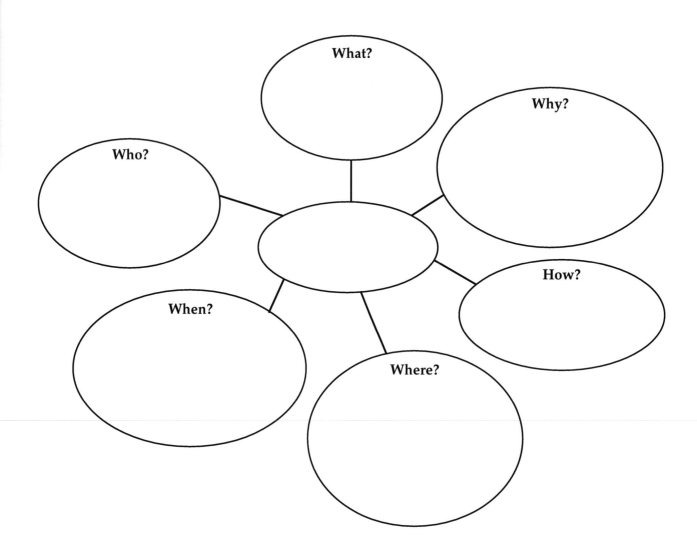

Main Idea and Details Chart

Write a supporting detail in each of the first three boxes. Write the main idea in the last box.

Supporting Detail:

+

Supporting Detail:

+

Supporting Detail:

=

The Main Idea:

Hierarchy Diagram

Write the most important element at the top of the chart. Write less important elements lower down. Use lines to show relationships between elements. Add or delete boxes and lines as needed to fit the material.

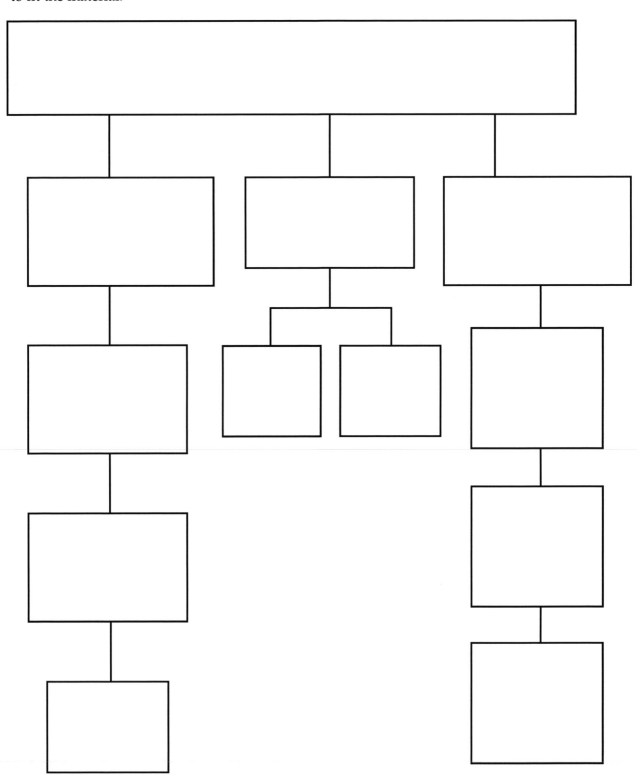

Spider Map

Write the topic or theme of the reading in the oval. Write one main idea on each diagonal line. Write one supporting detail on each horizontal line. Add or delete lines as needed.

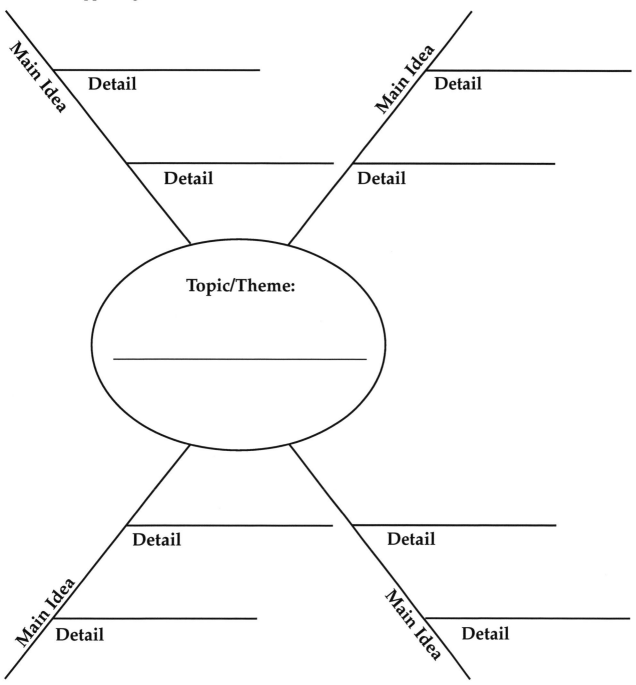

Time Line

Write events on the lines, with the earliest event at the bottom and later events, in order, on the upper lines. The most recent event should be at the top.

78

Sequence Chain

Write the first step or event in the first box. Write the other steps or events in order in the other boxes. Add or delete lines and boxes as needed.

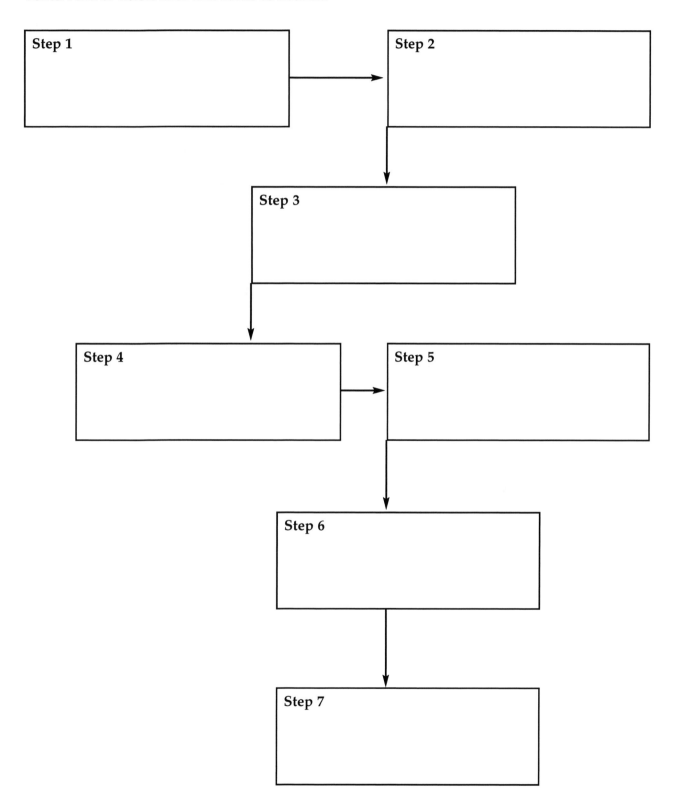

Step 1

Step 2

Step 3

Step 4

Step 5

Step 6

Step 7

Escalator Graph

An escalator graph is useful to show the steps in a process, much like a sequence chain. At the bottom of the escalator graph, write the beginning event. At the top, write the final outcome.

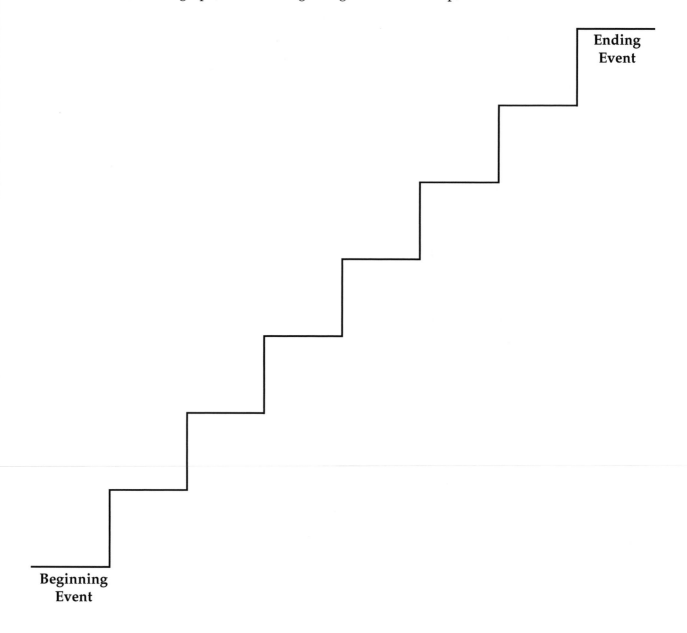

Ending Event

Beginning Event

Then and Now Chart

Write the topic you are charting at the top. Write the time periods you are comparing beside the words "Then" and "Now." Write information about the topic at each period on the appropriate side of the chart. Try to line up information in the same category—such as size, color, amount—on either side of the line to make comparing the two periods easier.

Topic: _____

Then: | **Now:**

Venn Diagram 1

Label both circles. Write similarities in the area where the circles intersect. Write differences in the areas where the circles don't intersect.

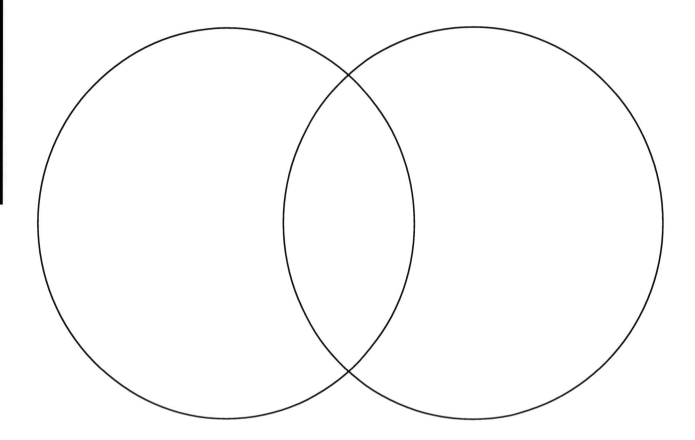

Venn Diagram 2

Label all three circles. Write similarities in the areas where the circles intersect. Write differences in the areas where the circles don't intersect.

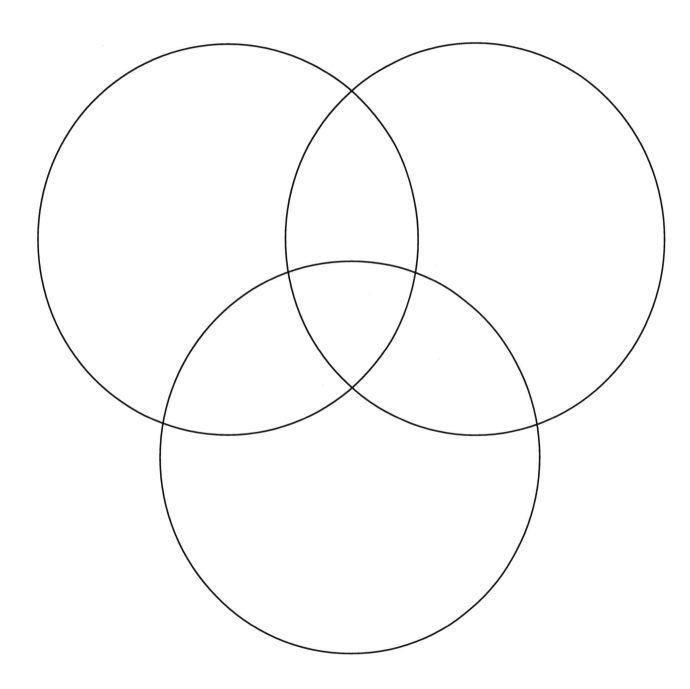

83

Comparison Matrix

Write the items you are comparing at the top of each column. Write one attribute at the start of each row. Add or delete rows and columns as needed.

Attribute 5 Name 1	Name 2
Attribute 1	
Attribute 2	
Attribute 3	
Attribute 4	

84

Cause and Effect Map

Write one cause in each oval. Write its effects in the rectangle that is connected to the oval.

Cause   ## Effect

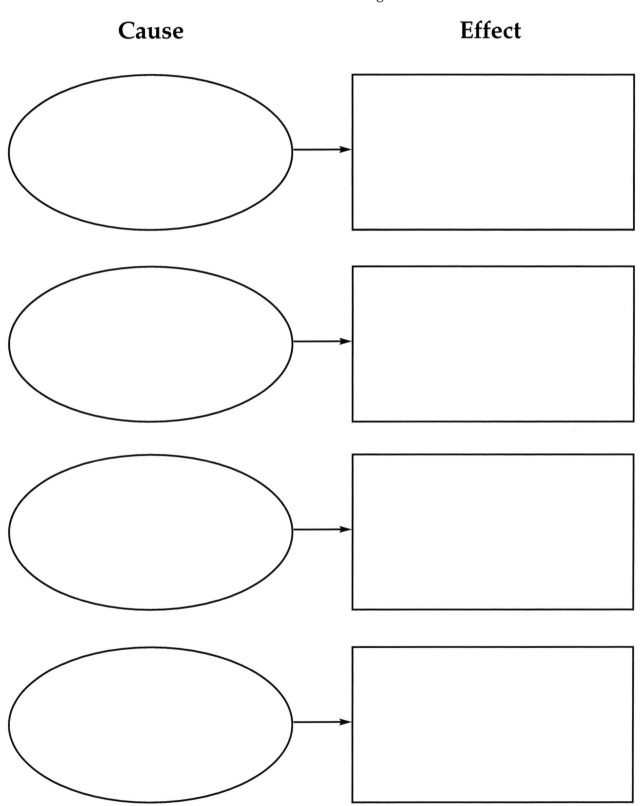

Problem/Solution Chart

Write the problem in the top box. Write the action taken to address the problem in the "Action" box. Write the results of the action in the "Results" box.

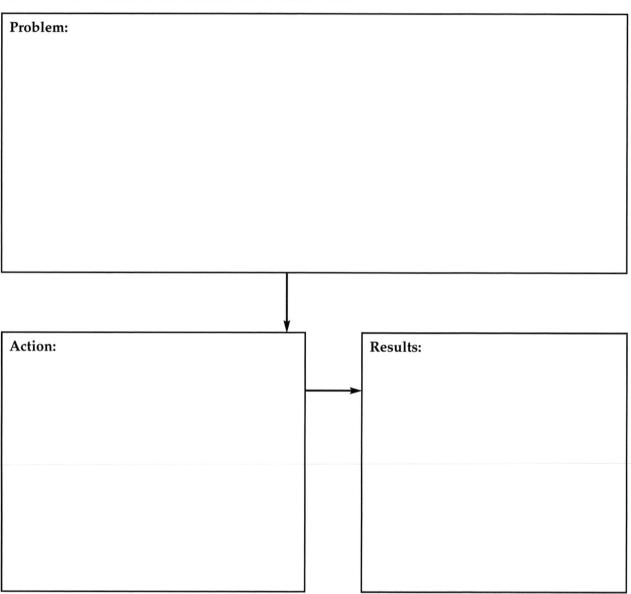

Problem:

Action:

Results:

Event Map

Write the event in the circle. Write a few words or a phrase in each box to show what happened, when it happened, where it happened, how it happened, why it happened, and who was involved.

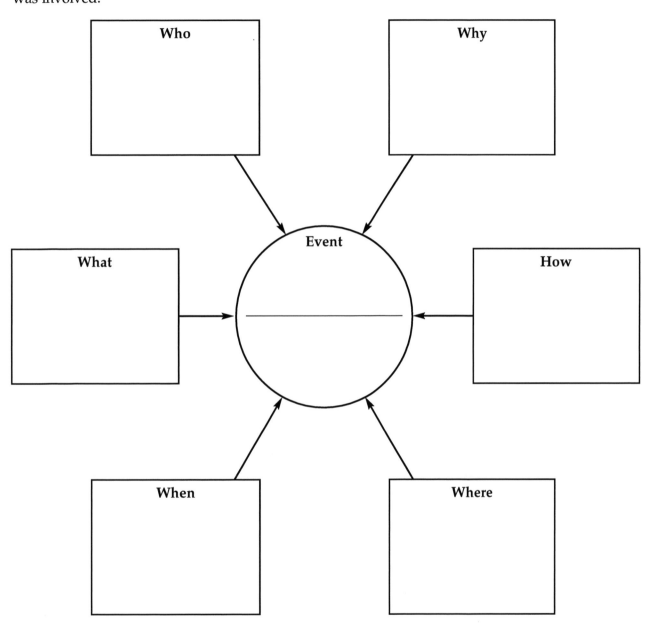

KWL Chart

Write your topic at the top of the chart. In the **K** part of the chart, write what you already know about the topic. In the **W** part of the chart, write any questions you have about the topic. Once you have done your research, write an overview of what you have learned in the **L** part of the chart.

Topic: _____

K What I KNOW	**W** What I WANT to Know	**L** What I LEARNED

Note-Taking Organizer

Write your research topic at the top. For each source you use, write the title, author, and other bibliographical details in the "Source" box. Write each note in a separate box. Include the page you found the information on at the top of the box. Don't copy word for word—just jot down key words and phrases. Add or delete boxes for sources and notes as needed.

Research Topic:			
Research Source 1 Author: Title:	Note: p. _____	Note: p. _____	Note: p. _____
Research Source 2 Author: Title:	Note: p. _____	Note: p. _____	Note: p. _____
Research Source 3 Author: Title:	Note: p. _____	Note: p. _____	Note: p. _____

Formal Outline

Write the title on the line at the top. Then fill in the rest of the outline with topics, subtopics, and supporting details. Add or delete lines as needed.

Title _____

I. Introduction

    A. Opening statement _____

                          _____

    B. Main idea or thesis _____

II. First major idea or topic _____

    A. Subtopic or clarifying idea _____

        1. Detail or example _____

        2. Detail or example _____

    B. Subtopic or clarifying idea _____

        1. Detail or example _____

        2. Detail or example _____

III. Second major idea or topic _____

    A. Subtopic or clarifying idea _____

        1. Detail or example _____

        2. Detail or example _____

    B. Subtopic or clarifying idea _____

        1. Detail or example _____

        2. Detail or example _____

IV. Conclusion _____

    A. Restatement of main idea _____

    B. Final statement _____

 # Informal Outline

Write your topic and thesis statement at the top. Write the statements that support the thesis statement in the boxes.

Topic: _____

Thesis statement:

Support Statement 1: Developed by:

Support Statement 2: Developed by:

Support Statement 3: Developed by:

Support Statement 4: Developed by:

Conclusion: Developed by:

Expository Writing Organizer

Use your outline to fill in the expository writing organizer. Add or delete sections as needed.

Opening Sentences:

Transition:

Paragraph 1 Topic sentence:

Supporting details:

Transition:

Paragraph 2 Topic sentence:

Supporting details:

Transition:

Paragraph 3 Topic sentence:

Supporting details:

Transition:

Conclusion:

Answer Key

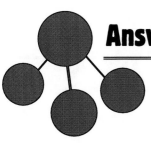

Answer Key: Lesson 2

Concept/Event Map, page 11
Answers will vary. Sample answer:

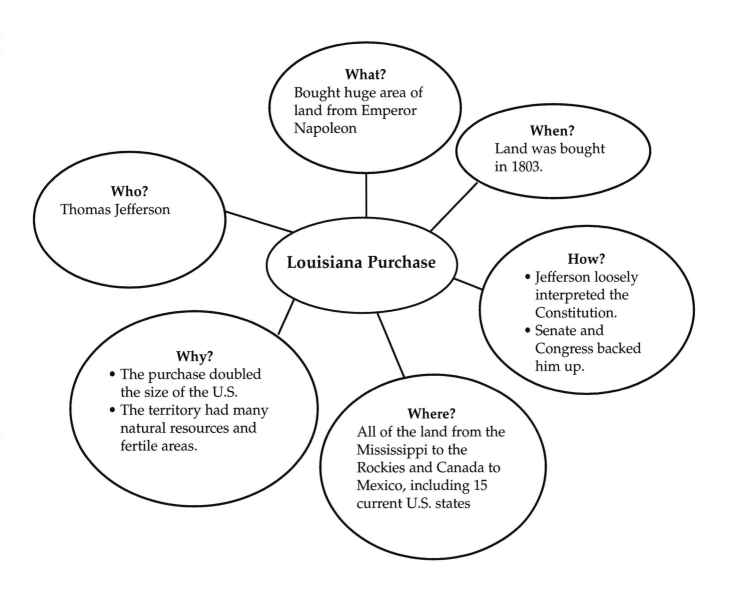

What?
Bought huge area of land from Emperor Napoleon

When?
Land was bought in 1803.

Who?
Thomas Jefferson

Louisiana Purchase

How?
• Jefferson loosely interpreted the Constitution.
• Senate and Congress backed him up.

Why?
• The purchase doubled the size of the U.S.
• The territory had many natural resources and fertile areas.

Where?
All of the land from the Mississippi to the Rockies and Canada to Mexico, including 15 current U.S. states

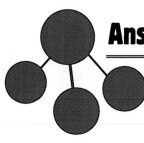

Answer Key: Lesson 2

Main Idea and Details Chart, page 16

Answers will vary. Sample answer:

Supporting Detail:
Lucy doesn't feel that working in the mill is hard work, especially since she will be there only a short time.

Supporting Detail:
Lucy thinks that if girls and women spend too much time at home, their view of the world becomes narrow.

Supporting Detail:
Being in the mill makes Lucy feel as if she is a part of a bigger human family.

The Main Idea:
Lucy describes her time working in the mill and says that it was a good experience.

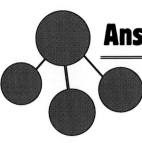

Answer Key: Lesson 2

Hierarchy Diagram, page 21
Answers will vary. Sample answer:

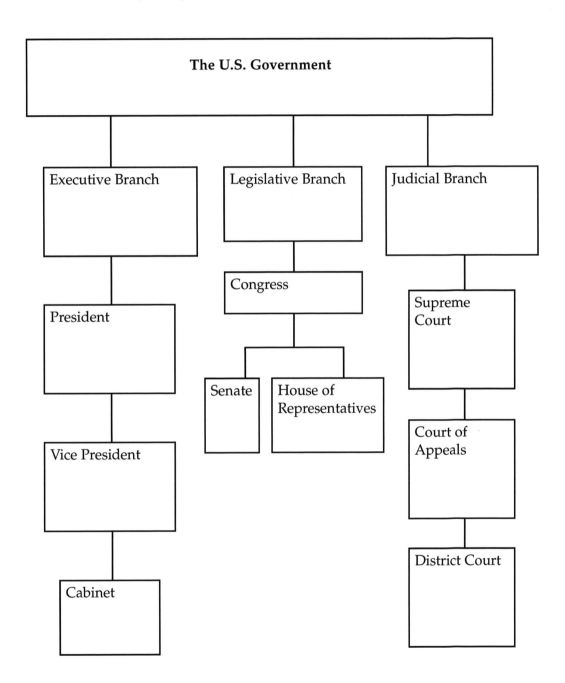

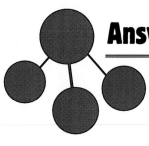

Answer Key: Lesson 3

Sequence Chain, page 32

Answers will vary. Sample answer:

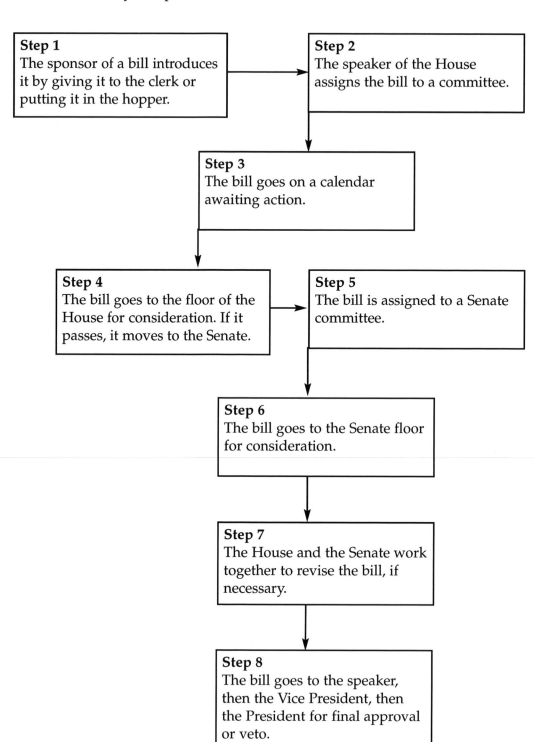

Step 1
The sponsor of a bill introduces it by giving it to the clerk or putting it in the hopper.

Step 2
The speaker of the House assigns the bill to a committee.

Step 3
The bill goes on a calendar awaiting action.

Step 4
The bill goes to the floor of the House for consideration. If it passes, it moves to the Senate.

Step 5
The bill is assigned to a Senate committee.

Step 6
The bill goes to the Senate floor for consideration.

Step 7
The House and the Senate work together to revise the bill, if necessary.

Step 8
The bill goes to the speaker, then the Vice President, then the President for final approval or veto.

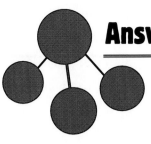

Answer Key: Lesson 4

Then and Now Chart, page 38

Answers will vary. Sample answer:

- What do I want to compare and contrast?
  Women's sports in Victorian times compared to today

- What do I want to learn about the things being compared or contrasted?
  How things are different today from Victorian times for women in sports

- What information do I need to have about both things in order to compare and contrast them?
  What details to include—should I also talk about women's dress?

- What did I learn? What did I discover by comparing and contrasting these things?
  That women were seen as delicate and that their femininity was very important. Also, that clothing determined the types of sports in which women participated.

Then (Victorian Age: 1837–1901)	Now
types of sports: croquet, archery, tennis, and golf	no restrictions
Only wealthy women played sports. Women weren't seen as powerful.	Sports are open to everyone. Power and muscles are seen as beautiful.
Bicycles began to change the way women moved and traveled.	Women ride bikes, play football, play baseball, and participate in other traditionally masculine sports.
Clothing for bikes became less restrictive.	Women wear whatever they want to participate in sports.

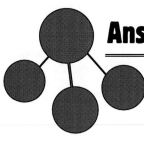

Answer Key: Lesson 4

Venn Diagram, page 42

Answers will vary. Sample answer:

Delaware

49th state in size

1,982 square miles

first state to
ratify Constitution

Named for the first governor
of Virginia, Lord de la Warr

Middle Atlantic state divided
by Mason-Dixon line

industries: chemical
products, food processing,
paper products

visiting spot:
Winterthur Museum

Both

small states

part of original
13 states

explored by Dutch

had strong Native American
cultures

have beautiful coastlines

have tourists visiting
the beaches

Rhode Island

ranks 50th in size

1,545 square miles

13th state to
ratify Constitution

named for the Greek island
Rhodes

part of New England

industries: jewelry-making,
tourism

Newport is home to
summer mansions

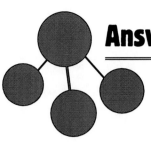

Answer Key: Lesson 5

Cause and Effect Map, page 48

Answers will vary. Sample answer:

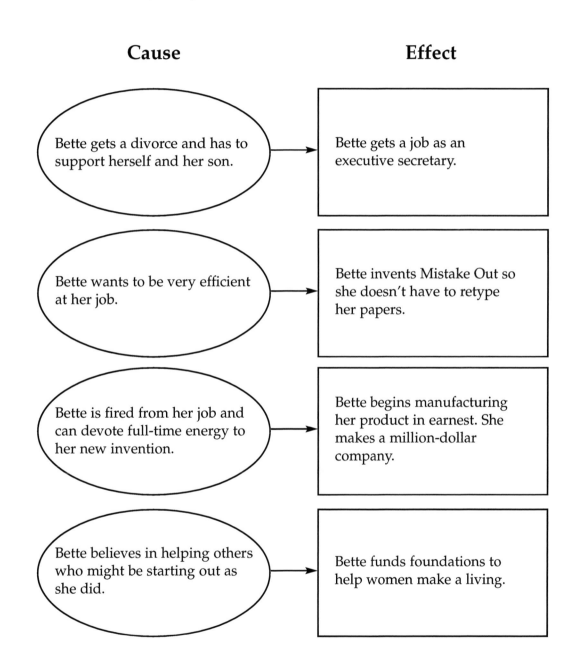

Cause	Effect
Bette gets a divorce and has to support herself and her son.	Bette gets a job as an executive secretary.
Bette wants to be very efficient at her job.	Bette invents Mistake Out so she doesn't have to retype her papers.
Bette is fired from her job and can devote full-time energy to her new invention.	Bette begins manufacturing her product in earnest. She makes a million-dollar company.
Bette believes in helping others who might be starting out as she did.	Bette funds foundations to help women make a living.

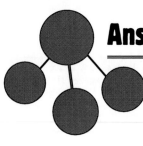

Answer Key: Lesson 5

Problem/Solution Chart, page 52

Answers will vary. Sample answer:

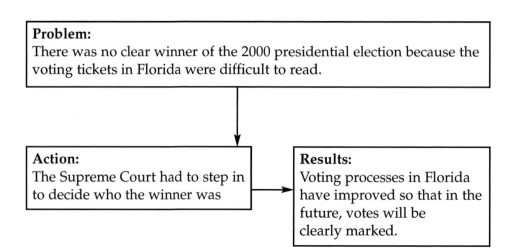

Problem:
There was no clear winner of the 2000 presidential election because the voting tickets in Florida were difficult to read.

Action:
The Supreme Court had to step in to decide who the winner was

Results:
Voting processes in Florida have improved so that in the future, votes will be clearly marked.

Share Your Bright Ideas

We want to hear from you!

Your name_____Date_____

School name_____

School address_____

City _____State _____Zip_____Phone number (_____)_____

Grade level(s) taught_____Subject area(s) taught_____

Where did you purchase this publication?_____

In what month do you purchase a majority of your supplements?_____

What moneys were used to purchase this product?

   ___School supplemental budget   ___Federal/state funding   ___Personal

Please "grade" this Walch publication in the following areas:

Quality of service you received when purchasing .... A   B   C   D

Ease of use.. A   B   C   D

Quality of content... A   B   C   D

Page layout .... A   B   C   D

Organization of material .... A   B   C   D

Suitability for grade level... A   B   C   D

Instructional value.. A   B   C   D

COMMENTS:_____

_____

What specific supplemental materials would help you meet your current—or future—instructional needs?

_____

Have you used other Walch publications? If so, which ones?_____

May we use your comments in upcoming communications?   ___Yes   ___No

Please **FAX** this completed form to **888-991-5755,** or mail it to

Customer Service, Walch Publishing, P. O. Box 658, Portland, ME 04104-0658

We will send you a **FREE GIFT** in appreciation of your feedback. **THANK YOU!**